DISOrientation

THE 13 "ISMS" THAT WILL SEND YOU
TO INTELLECTUAL "LA-LA LAND"

How to Go to College without Losing your Mind.

Edited by:

D1115806

ASCENSION PRESS

West Chester, Pennsylvania

Ascension Press
Post Office Box 1990
West Chester, PA 19380
Orders: 1-800-376-0520
www.AscensionPress.com

Cover design: Devin Schadt

Printed in the United States of America
10 11 12 13 14 6 5 4 3 2 1

ISBN 978-1-934217-94-8

To all those who over the centuries have toiled with neither glory nor reward passing along the works of the intellect, training young people in the liberal arts, and living the Faith of our fathers; to the monks who copied books and the sisters who taught the poor; to the scholars, artists, missionaries, and catechists; and to all honest seekers after truth.

Acknowledgments

We wish to thank each of the authors, who took time out of busy, busy schedules to examine these fundamental questions. Thanks to Faye Tatum Ballard, for her insightful comments on each of the early drafts, to Thomas More College of the Liberal Arts, to Intercollegiate Studies Institute, and to Matthew Pinto and the entire team at Ascension Press and their associates, including Leigh Brindley and Erica T. Rankin, for making this book a reality.

Contents

SENIOR DREAMWORLDS

BONUS ESSAY: COMMENCEMENT HERESY

A Syllabus of Errors

John Zmirak

This guide is meant as a kind of antidote to many of the books you probably will be assigned to analyze and regurgitate over the course of four years in college. Here you will find fourteen clear, digestible summaries of the ideologies you are likely to encounter in your classes across the curriculum—from English lit to biology, from economics to women's studies—and argue about with your friends over late night cups of coffee.

Each of the ideologies listed here is compelling, intriguing … and disastrously wrong. Much of the moral confusion and pointless bickering in the media comes from followers of one error (say, Scientism) facing off against the devotees of another (such as anti-Catholic fundamentalism). Or sometimes the fans of different, related heresies team up—for instance, when feminists and utilitarians cooperate to undermine the sanctity of life. Even college chaplaincies can be corrupted by these movements, for instance when they trade the Gospel for some trendy, toxic blend of Multiculturalism and Progressivism. And so on. If you drew up a Most Wanted list of the most dangerous ideas running loose today, you would find each one of them here.

None of these ideologies is completely, 100 percent wrong. If they were utter, obvious nonsense, then nobody would be taken in by them. Instead, every heresy amounts to a tiny piece of the truth, surgically removed from the rest of reality and grown in a test tube into a giant thumb, or ear, or tongue. When you try to reattach it to the body, it causes all sorts of problems because it throws everything out of balance. That's what ideologies do, with their fierce, fanatical focus. They narrow our vision, whip up our emotions, and tempt us to throw aside common sense, faith, and finally even logic. They are like intellectual drugs, and, yes, they can be addictive. This book is meant to save you the trouble of ending up in rehab.

Each of the authors is an expert in his or her field and has written longer, more academic works on the subjects tackled here. At the end of each essay, a recommended reading list points you to still more resources on each subject, of the sort you can cite in footnotes if you need to write a paper on one of these topics. (Watch out: Many professors don't appreciate it when you blast their unexamined premises out of the water, and your grade very well might suffer.)

We hope that you will delve into these books and these arguments—especially if you find yourself struggling with conflicts between the Faith you grew up with and the "bold new ideas" you will learn about in college. In fact, as you will see in each of these essays, none of these ideologies is really new; the intellectual trends that dominate most colleges aren't the fruit of social progress or real scientific inquiry. Instead, they are the result of old mistakes by philosophers, propaganda slogans coined by activists, or cop-outs on the part of cowardly prelates and politicians. Like the many layers of gloppy paint that you will find in old apartments, these accumulated mistakes obscure the underlying reality, and the only way to see the truth is to strip them away. That's what these essays do—they cut through the crud.

This pocket-sized map of intellectual landmines isn't meant to add to anyone's already intimidating reading lists. You don't need to write a essay about it, and it won't be on the exam—although the topics covered here will indeed make up the bulk of what you will be thinking and writing about throughout your college career. More importantly, the questions raised in this book are going to come up again and again throughout your life when you have make basic, real-world decisions. Your dating behavior will be affected by where you stand on Relativism, Hedonism, and Feminism. Your choice of career may hinge on how much you have been influenced by Consumerism and Cynicism. How you vote will be influenced by your attitude toward Sentimentalism, Americanism, Marxism, and Multiculturalism. Life and death medical decisions regarding your parents as they age will depend on where you stand on Scientism and Utilitarianism. The state of your soul when you die may hinge on how you have reacted to Progressivism, Modernism, and Anti-Catholicism.

As the great professor Richard M. Weaver once wrote in a book of the same title, "ideas have consequences." If you don't believe this, pay a visit to Iran or North Korea. Iranians and North Koreans aren't a different species, but their lives might look to us like something from a creepy science fiction movie. The reason? These societies are based on deeply mistaken ideas about human nature, human rights, and the nature of God. Since these ideas aren't fully true, or fully human, they don't treat people humanely. If we accept false ideologies, we will do the same thing, on a smaller scale. We will suffer, and so will the people around us, in this world and in the next.

Most of the ideologies the authors are warning you against don't present themselves as full-blown worldviews on the model of, say, Fascism or Islam. Instead, they insert themselves subtly into the unexamined assumptions people have learned to accept as "obviously" true. We hope that after reading these essays, you will know to be suspicious every time someone starts a sentence with one of the following phrases:

- As everybody knows…
- The educated consensus is…
- Of course, as everyone who isn't stuck in the Middle Ages realizes…
- All decent people agree…

Beginning an argument with such an appeal to popular opinion is a sure sign that someone's trying to put something over on you—to sell you a pack of undigested prejudice, which he probably hasn't even thought through himself. Peer pressure isn't something we outgrow in high school; in fact, it is the single most powerful force in shaping debates among professors and intellectuals. Most people don't want to be outsiders, and few faculty members wish to alienate the colleagues who will be voting on their promotions.

Each of these ideologies undermines clear thinking, disrupts society, and makes it harder to live a happy life. It is no coincidence that these heresies are also incompatible with the truth that sets us free. While errors are many and convoluted, the truth at its heart is simple. Christ is, as St. John wrote, the Logos, the principle of reason, thinking, and order inherent in the very essence of God. Whenever we find a piece of the truth—be it a principle of philosophy or the formula for the speed of light—we are in some sense encountering Christ. That is what sets the Christian Faith, which the Catholic Church teaches, apart from other religions. It is not some partial worldview or activist ideology, but rather the earthly shadow cast by the vast, unseen Reality that is God, who we will someday see face-to-face.

As we hope these essays show, in every case where ideologues assert that they have disproved some tenet of the Faith, it is their thinking that is faulty, partial, or dishonest. The same Church that saved the great books of the ancient world from destruction during the Middle Ages, that built the great cathedrals of Europe, whose missionaries serve the poor in every corner of the world, is also the Church for modern intellectuals. It sharpens our reason, gives hope to our hearts, and leads us out of the prison of selfishness. In the face of every philosophical fad, through twenty centuries, despite every kind of persecution, it has held fast to a richly complex vision of the Truth about God and man. The Church is never quite out of fashion because it has never been quite *in* fashion. There is always something about the Faith that rubs people the wrong way—and as society changes, its pet peeves about the Church change with it. As G.K. Chesterton wrote in his classic *Orthodoxy*, the Church was once seen as too pro-sex; now it is condemned as puritanical. The Church hasn't changed; the heresies have. And so they always will. The truth is the Rock that remains.

Freshman Errors

"In the absence of faith, we govern by tenderness,
and tenderness leads to the gas chamber."
– Flannery O'Connor, novelist and short story writer

Sentimentalism

Elizabeth Scalia

> Sentimentalism is an upbeat overemphasis on the
> inherent goodness of mankind that judges what is
> good or evil according to how well it accords with our
> feelings, or the feelings of people we want to impress.

If twentieth-century atheism rode in on the backs of totalitarian regimes, the twenty-first century has delivered unto the world an anti-God, anti-Church movement that fits seamlessly into shallow, postmodern popular culture. Having no need for uprisings and the hardware of destruction, the new fog of faith has crept in on the little cat feet of Sentimentalism, and it now sits on its haunches, licking its chops and congratulating itself.

Sentimentalism is the force behind "feel-goodism," the means by which we may cast off the conventions of faith and casually dismiss those institutions that refuse to submit to the trending times and morals. The sentimentalist trusts his feelings over hallowed authority or the urgings of his reason, frequently answering hard religious questions with some noble-sounding phrase like "the God I believe in wouldn't ..." (fill in the blank). What fits in that blank is typically some tenet of traditional faith that isn't currently fashionable, some moral demand that pop culture considers impossible—and hence, not worth even trying. Thus, the sentimentalist, while believing he follows the inviolate voice of his conscience, is really sniffing after trends, forming his heart according to the *sensus fidelium* of middlebrow magazines and public radio.

A sentimentalist cannot reconcile religious convictions—whether rooted in Scripture, tradition, or cultural practice—that do not correspond with his own considered feelings, which for him are both weighty and principled. Convinced that the people he loves cannot possibly be denied anything they want by a just God, or that the same just God would not permit deformities, illness, war, childhood abuse, or any of the human sufferings common to us all, he will not participate in a Church so fault-riddled and out-of-step with a generous and enlightened generation as ... his own.

I'm Too Good for the Church

That the churches are faulty is undeniable. The Catholic Church—indeed, much of Christianity—is an unkempt housemother to a den of miscreants. The place is teeming with gossips, adulterers, cheats, and liars—and that's just in the pews. Her leadership is, to the progressive perspective, irredeemably sexist, patriarchal, repressed, intolerant, and perhaps malevolent; it supposedly clings to outmoded tradition and outmoded thought due to a shrunken heart and— moderns suggest—an insufficient capacity to reason.

These charges are easy to make; they are full of modern buzzwords that suggest other buzzwords, and people use them as a sort of verbal shorthand, a social coding that denotes at which table one may sit in the societal lunchroom. They signal a bent of mind so "advanced" that it has done away with the need to reason and is content to let feelings and desires dress up as critical thought. Hence, a sentimentalist says he cannot reconcile himself to a Church that "holds women back"—a vague phrase used to signal support of women priests—while ignoring the historical evidence that Christianity helped women to "self-actualize" as no other society ever did. He says he cannot believe in a God who would "punish love" and, in this way, signals support for gay marriage, while brushing off pesky questions about physiology, covenants, or Scripture.

Of Sloppy Thinking and Loose Shoes

The sentimentalist uses such happy talk because it is inexact, squishy, and comfy, like an gel insert in a shoe. He willingly trades the clarity of ideas for the feeling that he (as opposed to you) is enlarged of heart and ennobled of mind. Nearly a hundred years ago, long before the sexual revolution, G.K. Chesterton wrote, "We can always convict [sentimentalists] by their weakness for euphemism. The phrase they use is always softened and suited for journalistic appeals. They talk of free love when they mean something quite different, better defined as free lust ... they insist on talking about birth control when they mean less birth and no control."[1]

Citing "irreconcilable differences," the sentimentalist divorces himself from the religious narrative; he takes a measure of the prevailing winds and then tries to shrink God and His Bride—the Church—into the narrow space of a fickle conventional wisdom. Conventional wisdom, of course, is often knee-jerk, seeing in every considered "no" an evidence of oppression, and every sin within the Church a proof of pervasive darkness.

Doubtless it would help if the Church itself were not such a refuge of sinners, both in the pews and in the robes. The disheartening failings of Church members and leaders lend credibility to a sentimentalist's declaration that he would rather spend his time with an honest sinner than a pious hypocrite. It is impossible to argue that a heterosexual priest who is unfaithful to his vows is preferable to a homosexual priest who is. The seemingly endless revelations of the clerical abuse of minors certainly makes a sentimentalist who casts off the Church in disgust seem more sensible than the equally-sickened Christian who remains within.

When the sentimentalist's reasonable outrage on behalf of very real victims inspires him to dissociate from the faith, he believes he has safely removed himself from the stains upon the Church. But, sadly, he has also made a decision to remove himself from the risks inherent in any measure of trust; that self-protective position may instruct him into a habit of rash judgment and narrow cynicism which can become crippling in other areas of life.

Though his anger at the Church and sympathy for the victims is indeed genuine, his unwillingness to participate in the broader sufferings of the Church entire—to face shame while hoping for clarity, to demand reforms while acknowledging the brokenness of humanity—ultimately denies him the growth that begins within the plumbed depths of shared humiliation, where grace may take root, and eventually grow into healing, strength, wisdom, and a peace that is frankly beyond the world's understanding.

I'm Spiritual ... Not Religious

Chesterton described the sentimentalist as one having "no honor about ideas; he will not see that one must pay for an idea as for anything else. He will not see that any worthy idea ... can only be won on its own terms."[2] That nicely describes the modern man who describes himself as "spiritual, not religious."

The sentimentalist, anxious to denounce and to distance himself, does not stop to consider that the great reformers within the Church—St. Francis, St. Teresa of Avila, St. Catherine of Siena, and others—did not flounce away from what was difficult. They remained, and the profound insights gained through their struggles have instructed and enhanced the "worthy idea" of faith. Dismissing it all with a few overused buzzwords, a sentimentalist runs his premium brain on the cheap and inefficient fuel of superior feeling, but he cannot be accounted a thinker who enhances understanding. And his destination is up for grabs, too.

The temptation to lapse into feeling-over-thinking is not unique to our century; it is simply the product of what we might call "Evian reasoning." This refers not to the boutique water whose name, read backwards, spells n-a-i-v-e (a happy irony), but reasoning that resembles the thought processes of Eve in the Garden, at the very infancy of human wondering. What sounds good and looks good must *be* good, and so we should have it, despite arguments to the contrary, or "arbitrary" rulings by an Authority. Eve allowed her imperfect reason to be subdued by her feelings and desires, and thus she took the world's headfirst dive into the waters of Sentimentalism, which—while shallow—are deep enough for infants to drown in.

The social mortification which the sentimentalist faces among his peers accounts for some of his conclusions, particularly as regards faith. By modern standards, the Church is asking him to bow down in fidelity before a God of embarrassingly retrograde positions, while the God he would prefer to worship bears such a striking resemblance to ... himself. *That* god thinks as he thinks, judges as he judges—and asks so very little of him, to boot. For him, the Church seems too black and white, lacking in the nuance that increasingly dulls the bright contrasts of ideas to bleak but soothing shades of gray. To his contemporaries, the Church that knows all life to be a sacred gift, and all babies to be blessings, is a brute who would suppress "a woman's right to choose," and inflict life upon the unwilling, the frightened, the victimized, and ... the very busy.

It's Supposed to be Easy, Isn't It?

The Church that suggests human beings are capable of containing their desires, and that the common call to chastity has both spiritual and social value, is an oppressor trying to keep people from expressing "free love" and ... feeling good about themselves through casual, empty encounters.

The Church that differentiates between the sexes and insists that each is indispensable to a divine plan meant to be carried out "in the fullness of time" is a mighty misogynist obsessing over form and function and "keeping women down."

The Church who understands that the Christ-instituted sacrament of marriage is a reflection of the Great Consummation of love between God and humankind, and who sees in this mystical union something that cannot be reduced to a mere matter of social justice, is an insecure homophobe, bowing down to men in dresses who want to foment hate, de-legitimize homosexual lives, narrow the expression of human love and ... just be mean for meanness' sake.

All of these arguments pit transcendent-if-challenging positions against less-exalted, unchallenging ideas that generally end in a splat of selfishness. The transcendent views—championing life, discipline, restraint, design, meaning, callings, union with God and eternity—belong to the Church. The other views—those that focus on the self and what the self wants and what the self demands—tend to be the sentimentalist's own views, soaked in from his peers and shared by the god of his making. On balance, they seem helplessly dull, short-sighted, stuck in time and beholden to illusion. Instead of urging individuals to their greatest potential, they teach there is nothing toward which we may reach at all, beyond the satisfaction of our here-and-now.

I'm Not a Judgmental Person

This emphasis on gratification and validation is a spiritual slight-of-hand; it convinces the sentimentalist that he is more *tolerant*, more *compassionate*, more interested in *supporting* humanity than is the Creator, and it undergirds that pretense by fomenting doubt. God may not celebrate the choices humans make with their gift of free will, but the sentimentalist does! In fact, thinks the sentimentalist, what sort of god would give people free will and then pass harsh judgment upon them when they use it? Only a very wicked, unloving god, or an illusion that is not a god at all.

In truth, the sentimentalist does not know what to think about God, whose invitation he has spurned, and whose study is only permitted in deconstruction, but he has heard enough to form an opinion: no loving god (or a god worth loving) he opines, could allow earthquakes and tsunamis, illness and grief, war and homelessness. He is unwilling to consider that a very loving (and praiseworthy) God inspires the sort of heroic rescue, relief, discovery, and responsive human aid that the sentimentalist admires.

The sentimentalist, who plays at positive thinking, is in fact a negativist. Instead of affirming the risks and sacrifices entailed in adult life, he holds his breath and tries to wish them all away.

The Power of Magical Thinking

Sentimentalism is the pretense of sophistication adopted by those who are so beholden to Cynicism (see essay 9), Relativism (see essay 2), or Hedonism (see essay 3) that they dare not risk a challenge to their worldview, and they would rather die than be thought out-of-touch. They believe themselves invulnerable to the "magical thinking" of faith by dint of their intellect, but they are paradoxically quite vulnerable to their society, at whose every pronounced trend and fickle philosophy they must subdue their own reason and adjust their opinions or risk an expulsion as absolute as Eve's was from Eden. The "dictatorship of relativism," against which Pope Benedict XVI has warned, wholly owns them and keeps them in a perpetual infancy of reason; under its stringent illusions, they believe they are unencumbered, wise and free. As then-Cardinal Ratzinger said in his homily at the Mass for the cardinals who were about to elect him pope:

> [T]he Son of God, true man [is] the measure of true humanism. Being an "Adult" means having a faith which does not follow the waves of today's fashions or the latest novelties. A faith which is deeply rooted in friendship with Christ is adult and mature. It is this friendship which opens us up to all that is good and gives us the knowledge to judge true from false, and deceit from truth. We must become mature in this adult faith; we must guide the flock of Christ to this faith. And it is this faith—only faith—which creates unity and takes form in love.[3]

A Church rooted in the truth is one that will dare to teach the Faith throughout the ages, rather than allow the ages to instruct the Faith.

The notion of a "dictatorship of relativism" is the blunt recognition that the subtle and not-so subtle pressure to conform to the age—and to the world—has become an overheated, will-sapping climate that demands comprehensive and non-negotiable obedience to the Zeitgeist: a surrender of thought, a surrender of reason, of individualism, identity and conscience. The Sentimentalism that D. H. Lawrence described as "the working off on yourself of feelings you haven't really got,"[4] demands the habitual redressing of the old man in the latest fashion, and bleakly denies that a new man may ever be put on. It sets one upon an unstable pathway, where stones are yanked out from under one's feet because they suddenly do not fit, or are needed elsewhere to bolster another idea.

Childlike or Childish?

By repeating Benedict's exhortations to maturity, am I suggesting that the sentimentalist is immature, or childlike? Well, yes and no. There is no shame in being immature unless one steadfastly insists on remaining so, simply because it is expedient. But to be childlike is different from being childish. The first denotes a quality of innocent trust that one cannot cultivate while committed to cynicism and doubt, which is where the sentimentalist resides. Children are not cynics, and they push doubt away with both hands because they want to believe. They know that without belief, there is nothing to hold on to but time, which is an illusion.

The world is a dangerous and complicated place in which the Church, populated and served by those flawed and faulty humans who seek their redemption in the worship of something greater than themselves, survives wholly through grace of the Holy Spirit. But the fact that it does still survive should indicate, as mankind cannot, God's presence within it.

Ultimately, our lives within the world and within the Church are between ourselves and God. One can stave off Sentimentalism by resisting the urge to get so caught up in the forest of trends and ideas that one cannot locate the Tree of Life which is the Church, or be nourished by its fruit, which has largely built and sustained the very culture some now believe has grown in wisdom by sawing off its own roots.

Elizabeth Scalia is a contributing writer to First Things *(where she also blogs as The Anchoress) and is a regular panelist on the Brooklyn Diocese-produced current events program,* In the Arena, *seen at netny.net. She is also the Catholic "portal manager" at www.patheos.com.*

Recommended Reading

√ *Survivals and New Arrivals*, by Hilaire Belloc (Charlotte: TAN Books, 1993).

√ *The Faithful Departed*, by Philip Lawler (New York: Encounter Books, 2008).

√ *Conversion: The Spiritual Journey of a Twentieth-Century Pilgrim*, by Malcolm Muggeridge (Eugene, OR: Wipf & Stock Publishers, 2005).

√ *Mystery and Manners*, by Flannery O' Connor (New York: Farrar, Straus and Giroux, 1969).

√ *The Thanatos Syndrome*, by Walker Percy (New York: Farrar, Straus and Giroux, 1999).

Notes

1 From his essay "Obstinate Orthodoxy," in *The Thing* (1929); published in *The Collected Works of G.K. Chesterton* (San Francisco: Ignatius Press, 1990).

2 Be sure to read the whole essay! "The sentimentalist," in *The Wit, Whimsy, and Wisdom of G. K. Chesterton, Volume 5*, by G.K. Chesterton (Landisville, PA: Coachwhip Publications, 2009). See also "On the Alleged Optimism of Dickens," *Charles Dickens*, by G.K. Chesterton (Kelly Bray, UK: House of Stratus, 2001).

3 Homily, April 18, 2005. For full text see *www.vatican.va/gpII/ documents/homily-pro-eligendo-pontifice_20050418_en.html* .

4 Read this in context in "John Galsworthy," *Study of Thomas Hardy and Other Essays*, by D.H. Lawrence (New York: Cambridge University Press, 1985).

"We are moving toward a dictatorship of Relativism which does not recognize anything as for certain and which has as its highest goal one's own ego and one's own desires."
– Pope Benedict XVI

RELATIVISM

Eric Metaxas

> Relativism is the assertion that truths, especially moral truths, have no validity independent of the "values" treasured by the person or society that asserts them.

I first encountered Relativism when I went to college at Yale. Before that, I had lived in a working-class world in middle America, where truth was a real concept. In my parents' world, truth was something noble and beautiful; it was something that people lived and died for, like freedom. To be an enemy of the truth was to be about the worst thing there was. Since Yale's motto is *Lux et Veritas*—Latin for "Light and Truth"—I was eager to get there so that I could begin learning what truth really was. I was genuinely excited about the idea of searching for it.

But by the time I got there in the 1980s, Yale had abandoned the outdated notion that truth was something real, something to be sought after, discovered, and treasured. By then, that one-time seminary in New Haven had, as preachers like to say, "backslidden." Yale had fully espoused a winking, post-modern attitude, in which the notion of a singular truth had been replaced by the relativistic theory that there are many "truths"—or no truths at all. I felt disappointed, like someone in the desert who sees an oasis and runs toward it, only to find it vanished once he gets there. Truth was all just a mirage. Happily, my fellow students offered me something to replace it.

"Celery Green" Day

At Yale, I began to hang out with a group of friends who were politically and theologically liberal. They tended toward a relativistic view of the world, and I began to see things as they did. (This happens *a lot* in college.) One of my friends had even invented a holiday that was a celebration of Relativism. He called it "Celery Green" Day.

And this is how he explained it: Every spring, as you look out over the landscape of trees in your particular neck of the woods, the wash of colors slowly changes from gray to green. In Connecticut, where I grew up and where Yale is located, the dull wintry granite gray of the bare tree branches was unchanged for months, as though the trees really had died and had turned to stone. But finally, at some point, tiny red buds appeared and the trees would from a distance take on the slightest reddish hue. Then, some days or weeks later, the faintest suggestion of spring would arrive in a hint of yellow green. This was usually in April. That implicit hint of budding color would become more explicit each day until one day, looking out over the hills or trees, one saw a luminescent optic yellow-tinged green that was the approximate color of a celery stalk. This, dear reader, was known as Celery Green Day.

The color would soon deepen, so the actual color of celery green usually only persisted for a few days. But only the first day on which this color appeared was Celery Green Day. You had to be paying attention, or you would miss it! At the time, I thought Celery Green Day a beautiful idea, and, in many ways, I still do.

But for us liberally-minded students, the real charm of Celery Green Day was its utterly radical subjectivity. It could fall on *any* day, so no one could know when it would arrive. It was a holiday that showed up unannounced, whenever it pleased. So planning a Celery Green Day celebration was essentially impossible. At best, it was a guessing game. And the subjectivity doesn't stop there. I might determine that Celery Green Day had arrived on Tuesday, but you might say that the trees hadn't been quite green enough. As far as you were concerned, they hadn't really turned to actual celery green until Thursday. Another friend might say Friday. But who was right? That was the point: *There was no right answer.* Everyone was equally correct. We all had our own "truths" and that was that. Celery Green Day was the holiday where one's own subjectivity reigned supreme!

But the subjectivity went further still. Even to the same person, Celery Green Day would be different from town to town and valley to valley and state to state. The foliage and weather in one place would be different than the foliage and weather in another place, so even by my own reckoning, Celery Green Day on Stony Hill in Danbury, where I grew up, would fall on a different day than Celery Green Day in New Haven, where I was going to school. You could probably throw your worldly possessions into a VW bus and, like a Dead Head, follow Celery Green Day north from place to place for weeks on end. What a trip that would be. *Like, don't bogart that joint, dude!*

Celery Green Day was the very essence of freedom from constraints and rules. It was ungraspable ... it was indefinable ... Celery Green Day was like that girl from art history class with unshaven legs and bits of leaves and granola in her uncombed hair—all free and easy. And completely undemanding. It was capricious and untethered, gamboling across the hills, mau-mauing the Dead White Males who dared declare anything to be concrete and specific and historical. Celery Green Day was a fresh-faced *printemps*-heralding goddess of *Liberté, Égalité,* and *Fraternité.* In her very freedom and ungraspability she was sticking it to the Man! Take that, Christopher Columbus, with your silly historical dates and facts and oppressive attitudes toward indigenous peoples!

What is Truth?

So much for Celery Green Day. The problem with such a celebration is that accepting its general premise somehow drains the life out of other holidays. Each one of them is based on a real event, which took place on a certain date because real human beings once really thought that they were working, fighting, or dying for something true. (July Fourth leaps to mind; also Good Friday.) If we want to mark any of them, we have to come back to the question of questions:

What is truth? But we have to ask it differently than Pontius Pilate asked it. There's no question that it's a difficult question.

Defining truth is a lot like defining light or love or God. It's not easy. For example: Is love a verb or a noun? Is light a particle or a wave? Was Jesus God or man? Was the Bible written by people or by God?

When you're talking about the most profound things in the universe, the answer is almost always *both*. Love is a verb *and* a noun. Light is particles *and* waves. Jesus was fully God *and* fully man. And since the Bible was written by people *inspired by the Holy Spirit,* it was written by God *and* by men. Truth is just like that. It is infinitely complex and infinitely simple at the same time—and have I mentioned that it is seemingly paradoxical in its very essence? Truth is both verb and noun. It's feminine and masculine. It's law, but it's also grace and forgiveness for those who break the law.

Because truth is so hard to define, some people tend to take a shortcut and opt for what amounts to a half-truth—an oversimplified version of truth, which is not truth at all. They usually give you a false choice between *two* half-truths. Each one is a counterfeit version of truth. Relativism is one of them; the other is authoritarianism or fundamentalism. So Relativism really isn't anti-truth. It's anti-authoritarian and anti-fundamentalist. *Relativism is a confused idea of what truth really is.*

A relativist sets up the straw man of authoritarianism and fundamentalism in the place of actual truth—and then tries to knock it down. What the relativist is really saying is that he has a deeper truth than all of those authoritarians and fundamentalists who talk about truth. Relativists believe that truth is more like a verb than a noun, more like a flower than a rule, more like a butterfly than a bullet. Like a butterfly, it flits here and there and is free and fragile, and it eschews the ugly, dull, and violent purposefulness of a bullet.

So relativists don't understand that there is really such a thing as truth. They pretend that the only other option to Relativism is authoritarianism and fundamentalism. If you want to talk about truth—or, God forbid, about Truth—they immediately label you an authoritarian or a fundamentalist or (even worse!) an angry, patriarchal white male. They will likely suggest that you have violent and oppressive tendencies. Even if you don't ever do anything but talk, they will suggest that your talking that way will lead to violence—and secretly wants to incite violence. In their conversations on this subject, relativists tend to play the violence card early and often. They are sincerely threatened by the idea of truth. To them, it is inherently militaristic and masculine. Talk about truth in the singular, and to some people your face and features will start to morph into an ugly caricature.

"Dance of the Macabre Mice"

If Celery Green Day typified the notion of Relativism while I was at Yale, the quintessential illustration of the authoritarian and fundamentalist idea of truth came from a Wallace Stevens poem we read in class called "Dance of the Macabre Mice." In the poem of that title, Stevens writes sarcastically about an equestrian statue of some military hero, holding an outstretched sword. Just as Celery Green Day was like a verb—whimsical and light and unpredictable and free—the equestrian statue was a dead noun, heavy and hostile and full of itself. One was somehow feminine, or Feminist. The other was the typical Feminist's picture of the stereotypical male.

Stevens depicts the equestrian statue not as heroic and glorious, but as militaristic and oppressive. In the poem, mice crawl all over the statue and then "dance out to the tip of Monsier's sword." They are light-footed and victorious in their battle with the dead equestrian hero. "What a beautiful tableau," the poem declares with archness and irony, "The arm of bronze outstretched against all evil!" It's not just mocking the idea of heroism, but the very idea of goodness and evil. For, according to the relativist, these too are outdated notions.

To the relativist, all truths are as outdated and ironic as Stevens' statue. The beautiful idea that we are created in the image of God, and that every human being is therefore sacred, is also unacceptable. If pressed, many or even most relativists prefer to think of us as just part of a broad evolutionary continuum, not much different than apes or cockroaches. They see everything as relative and as part of a continuum. The child in the womb is less valuable than the child outside the womb, and the person in a coma is less valuable than the person who is healthy. The idea that human life is inherently sacred, at every stage, they find simply incomprehensible. They do not "get" it.

In the Garden of Eden, the Serpent put doubt into Eve's mind about what God had said. "Did God *really* mean ...?" The slogan "Question Authority" plays the same role in modern society: it is Relativism at the level of the bumper sticker. That slogan doesn't suggest that we should question authority to determine if that authority is legitimate. It states that *all* authority is suspect—and hence, all assertions about the truth.

The relativist, like Pontius Pilate, is world-weary and cynical, and when he asks "What is truth?", he is not really seeking an answer. As far as he is concerned, there is none. The question is not asked hopefully and openly, but cynically and sadly.

In his magnificent Nobel Prize acceptance speech in 1970, Alexander Solzhenitsyn quoted a famous Russian proverb: "One word of truth outweighs the world." Truth is the thing that makes evil dictators tremble; it is the thing that can never lose, that cannot long be suppressed, that according to Shakespeare "will out," sooner or later. Eventually it must arise from the darkness and be victorious. God created the world this way. Truth always wins out. But to all of these noble ideas, and to the concepts of good and evil themselves, the relativist ... shrugs. Or winks.

The Christian View of Truth

Just as light is not just a wave and not just a particle, but both— so truth is neither relativistic nor fundamentalist but partakes of a little bit of each. In other words, it has room for equestrian statues and shades of celery green. Jesus was no authoritarian or fundamentalist, but neither was He a relativist. He showed grace to the woman taken in adultery and did not condemn her, as the Pharisees did. But then He said to her: "Go and sin no more." He didn't wink at sin; He admonished it and then forgave it.

The Bible does not take a heavy-handed authoritarian view of truth—though many misread it that way. But it does take truth extremely seriously. In its pages, God Himself claims to *be* the truth.

Jesus said: "I am the Way and the Truth and the Light" (John 14:6). That's precisely because Jesus is the perfect balance between these two half-truth versions of the truth. Genuine truth walks a tightrope. Relativism falls off the tightrope to the left and authoritarianism/ fundamentalism falls off it to the right, but both fall into the same abyss, while truth takes our breath away by walking the tightrope.

So Christians cannot be authoritarians or fundamentalists. The Bible condemns the Pharisees, who were full of moral rules and judgment but had no love and grace for those who struggled morally. To wield truth like a sword leads to pharisaism and moralism. Islamo-fascism, of course, exemplifies this approach to truth.

But unlike the relativist, we cannot shrug at truth. Christians believe in moral laws and in doctrine. We declare that "Jesus is Lord." We say that Jesus died and then rose from the grave. We believe that Jesus is God. We believe in a moral order and in rules about how we are to conduct ourselves, physically and otherwise. We believe marriage is sacred and adultery is wrong. Relativism is profoundly uncomfortable with such blanket assertions. But Christians do not *only* believe in moral laws and in doctrine. We believe in a Person. And that Person said He *was* Truth.

So the relativist only wants to talk about grace, and the authoritarian or fundamentalist only wants to talk about the law. But truth is a Person who insists we talk about both. Truth is a Person who exemplified a perfectly moral life, and who also died so that those of us who would fail to lead morally perfect lives could be with Him forever in paradise.

Anyone who would turn truth into authoritarianism or Relativism has to look at Jesus to see a living example of what truth really is, in all its multi-dimensional glory. People who try to turn the God of the Bible into an authoritarian figure who merely thunders judgment need to *look at Jesus*, who forgives, to see that they only have half the truth, and therefore none. And people who try to turn Jesus into a relativist who merely forgives without judging (since sin is no big deal) need to see that the whole point of His coming to earth was to die on the cross so that He could pay for our sins. That makes sin a very big deal indeed.

Just before Pontius Pilate asks Jesus "What is truth?", Jesus says that He Himself came into the world to testify to the truth. He also says that everyone on the side of truth listens to Him. To Pilate and to the modern relativist, Jesus' statements seem arrogant or insane. And if they weren't true, they certainly would be arrogant or insane. But there is good news: they actually *are* true. And that's the truth.

Eric Metaxas is author of the New York Times *best-sellers* Bonhoeffer: Pastor, Martyr, Prophet, Spy *and* Amazing Grace: William Wilberforce and the Heroic Campaign to End Slavery. *He is the founder and host of* Socrates in the City. *For more information, visit* www.ericmetaxas.com.

Recommended Reading

√ *Escape from Scepticism,* by Christopher Derrick (San Francisco: Ignatius Press, 2001).

√ *The Abolition of Man,* by C.S. Lewis (New York: HarperOne, 2001).

√ *Chance or the Dance,* by Thomas Howard (San Francisco: Ignatius Press, 1989).

√ *An Introduction to Philosophy,* by Jacques Maritain (Lanham, MD: Rowman & Littlefield Publishers, 2005).

√ *Everything You Always Wanted to Know About God ... But Were Afraid to Ask,* by Eric Metaxas (Colorado Springs, CO: Waterbrook Press, 2005).

"Oh, how desperately bored, in spite of their grim determination to have a Good Time, the majority of pleasure-seekers really are!"
– Aldous Huxley, author, *Brave New World*

HEDONISM

John Zmirak

> Hedonism is the belief that the pursuit of pleasure—
> intellectual, emotional, or physical—and the avoidance
> of suffering ought to guide human decisions.

People say that it's fun to be young. People say a lot of things. Middle-aged parents and teachers have probably told you things like, "These are the best years of your life—make the most of them!" College calendars are stuffed with enough events to grind the hardiest party animal into a pile of motionless sawdust, and for once your parents aren't around to set deadlines, dole out spending money, sniff your breath or clothes for "substances," or otherwise babysit you. If you're living away at school, this is the most independence you've ever had. You've got cash and a flexible schedule (all those books won't read themselves, but the end of semester seems years away and you've always been good at cramming).

From watching your parents, you are pretty sure that middle age is a snore: If there is any time you are going to really enjoy life, college seems to be it. This is your one window of opportunity to really cut loose, sow some oats, have wild romances with people you wouldn't normally fool with, and in general live the way those maniacs do in college movies you've been watching since you turned thirteen. You might even feel a duty to get "out there" and see what happens. Indeed, if you aren't having as good a time as you feel you're expected to, you will actually feel guilty.

Is this vague sense one has at a certain age the moral obligation to spit beer all over the wall the same thing as Hedonism? Certainly, they are connected. If your expectations of college life are similar to those we have just mentioned, you are likely to engage in some pretty seriously hedonistic behavior—and no, it won't turn out to be as much fun as it does in the movies. The director usually cuts away before the drunk "girl gone wild" gets sick and starts sobbing in the corner, or the stoner dude flunks out of school and ends up dunking fries at McDonald's in between twelve-step meetings.

Still, the *Animal House* mentality hardly rises to the level of a heresy that would rate inclusion in this kind of book, alongside such deadly poisons as Relativism (see essay 2) and Feminism (see essay 10). Such misbehavior—and the fantasies people have of the really *awesome* naughty fun other folks must *somewhere* be having, if only we could get invited to their parties—can largely be chalked up to people being immature and easily led. If someone's ideas on how to spend four whole years of his life, and a huge chunk of his parents' money, have actually been formed by repeated viewings of *Old School*, his problem isn't really philosophical. He just needs to grow up—and let's hope he does before he catches an incurable disease, wrecks his liver, marries a maniac on a whim, drunk-drives into a school bus, or fathers an "unwanted child" whose survival is uncertain.

Many glamorous figures in the arts have seemed to live according to such a degraded ethic. We still remember "great lovers" like Casanova and Lord Byron, tough guys like Ernest Hemingway and Norman Mailer, romantic rebels against convention like James Joyce and D.H. Lawrence—and that's not even getting into the world of popular music, where jazz players and rock singers blazed whole new trails in search of "extreme experiences." There's nothing that will boost an artist's reputation like his willingness to challenge "stale, bourgeois conventions" of right and wrong—which is I guess what author William Burroughs was doing when he drunkenly played "William Tell" with an apple on top of his wife's head. She died, but it happened down in Mexico, so feminist critics give him a pass.

The mindless pursuit of short-term pleasure at any cost is the best way to describe the phenomenon we now know as addiction. Cocaine offers anyone who snorts a little powder the same feeling he would have if he had won the world's most attractive spouse, beaten his enemies to death with his Academy Award, then carried his bride up Mount Everest. All this, from a little snort of powder. No wonder such abuse wears out the "pleasure centers" in the brain, which soon require regular doses of drugs just to keep the addict out of clinical depression. Casual sex works much the same way, greedily grabbing the ecstasy our body offers as a reward for forming a lasting, loving relationship and procreating the species.

Hedonism: Suffering is a Miscalculation

But there is no point in making a philosophical argument against selfish and self-destructive behavior. There is something more serious going on when we talk about Hedonism, a worldview that makes coherent claims about the nature of man and his bodily existence, the meaning of suffering, and the ethical standards that should guide our behavior all through our lives—not just in our leisure time or in college. There have been serious thinkers throughout history who have argued for what boils down to Hedonism.

Epicurus is the most famous, and since his very name has come to be a synonym for "really good restaurant," his arguments deserve our careful scrutiny. Epicurus rejected as unproveable Plato's assertion that the transient objects we see before our eyes—such as rocks, trees, and let's be candid, each other—are actually imperfect earthly copies of timeless "forms" that exist (as we might put it today) in the mind of God. Instead, Epicurus held what we might recognize as an almost modern view: The world and everything in it is simply composed of tiny particles called "atoms," which make up each one of us for the brief period of time that we actually exist. At some point, those atoms will fall apart, and we will dissolve into nothingness, and that's the end of the story. Epicurus' views were taken up again by the Roman writer Lucretius, whose *De Rerum Natura* ("On the Nature of Things") put the Epicurean theory of "atomism" into the form of an epic poem.

Now, Epicurus didn't preach a gospel of party-hearty, live-for-the-moment sensualism. No educated Greek would have favored something like that—and if he had, his views would be easy to dismiss. Indeed, Epicurus argued that pleasure was the only real good and pain the only evil, but he knew enough about life to see that the animalistic pursuit of instant gratification was pragmatically counterproductive. You can't very well go around stealing food off other's people's plates just because you're hungry or forcing unwilling partners into bed. If you do, you will quickly end up suffering a great deal more pain than any pleasure you might have enjoyed. (Looters might have fun smashing windows and stealing appliances, but their chances for gratification will be radically curtailed once they are locked up in prison.) So Epicurus advised that people practice self-control and delayed gratification, prudently calculating how to gain the greatest pleasure over the long run. This is the principle behind all those "safe sex" seminars you were offered during Freshman Orientation— the trick is to get the highest possible ratio of orgasms to unwanted pregnancies or STDs. The one who dies with the most joys "wins."

Put this way, Epicurus's views appear less eccentric—in fact, they sound eerily like the way most modern secular Westerners plan and live their lives. Here is an easy way to spot a modern Epicurean: It's anyone who uses the phrase "consenting adult" in any context whatsoever. The most famous American Epicurean thinker was founding father Thomas Jefferson, who followed the Enlightenment impulse to reject revealed Christianity and reach back behind it to more "rational" Classical models. (As president, Jefferson tipped his hand: He rewrote the New Testament, editing out all the miracles and prophecies—leaving behind a curious collection of dubious advice given by a wandering Jewish carpenter with no particular competence or authority. This book was printed and distributed at U.S. government expense.)

Stoicism: Suffering is Radio Static

The Epicureans weren't teaching in a vacuum. They faced serious philosophical competitors. Beside the Platonists (who would educate St. Augustine before his conversion) were the Stoics, who believed in a distant, inscrutable God who ruled the world through the irresistible force that they called Fate. It was God's realm of spirit that was *really* real, while the "lower" world of bodies, rocks, and broccoli was an illusion—even a snare.

The Stoics taught that whatever suffering we endure in life is part of that illusion. Even the emotions of suffering or enjoyment are fundamentally fantasies; the lasting core or essence of each person is his reason—and as long as you have that faculty, you are free to focus your mind on the "higher" things, like philosophy and mathematics. Whether you are locked in a dark, dank prison, starving in a camp, or undergoing torture shouldn't matter to you one whit—any more than you should let your head be turned by pleasure or success. The greatest Stoic writer was the Roman emperor Marcus Aurelius, whose *Meditations* displayed his cool detachment from the absolute power and infinite perks that came with his office. Instead of indulging himself like some of his more decadent predecessors (Nero and Caligula come to mind), Marcus Aurelius sternly focused his mind on his civic duties, urging his readers (and subjects) to do the same.

Gnosticism: Suffering Comes from the Evil God

The other important contenders for the minds of ancient Romans and Greeks were the groups who called themselves Gnostics (which roughly translates as either "the smart guys" or "the know-it-alls"). Like the Stoics and the Platonists, the Gnostics held that the world of the body is fundamentally meaningless. They went even further, and declared that the body is, in fact, evil.

It is easier to understand how people might come to such a conclusion in an age before modern hygiene, painkillers, or any effective medicine. Looking at spiders, maggots, vultures, and even "noble" predators like the lion, and considering the pain of childbirth and the transitory nature of earthly life, the Gnostics concluded that whatever was behind the material world, it wasn't our friend. In fact, the Gnostics taught, the earth was the creation of lesser demonic spirits ... essentially fallen angels.

According to the Gnostics, the One God was not directly accessible, but had to be approached through an elaborate hierarchy of intercessory spirits—the nature of which was secret, and could only be transmitted to a tiny elite of "knowers" through mystic rituals. In other words, Gnosticism was a whole lot like Greco-Roman voodoo. It was a Gnostic sect called Manichaeism that Augustine fell into in his youth. Gnostic notions would re-emerge in the Middle Ages in southern France with the Albigensian movement, and were only finally wiped out by a brutal crusade.

For Gnostics, bodily pleasures such as sex were fundamentally evil and should be renounced—but if you couldn't manage that, at the very least you should avoid marriage and children. Adultery and abortion were preferable, the former since at least it avoided the pretense of sanctity, and the latter because it spared fresh souls from being trapped in the prison of the flesh.

These were the philosophical systems that the early Church had to contend with, and it is not surprising that converts to the Church sometimes carried baggage with them from the schools they had left behind. What is more, Christian apologists—those who offered rationales for the Faith to outsiders—had to use philosophical language that was familiar to the people whom they addressed. So they would draw on Platonic or Stoic ideas of self-restraint and rationality when addressing thoughtful pagans. While neither of these philosophical systems was fully compatible with what the Church taught about suffering, the material world, or the fact that God had become incarnate in the flesh of Jesus Christ, at least they directed men to lives of discipline and spiritual inquiry. Of course, Christians had to reject Gnosticism altogether, since the whole point of God becoming man was that the Creator of the universe had come to reclaim and sanctify the world He had (in Genesis) called "good."

Christianity: Suffering Can Be Redemptive

The other worldview that Christians had to attack head on was Epicureanism. Why? Because of an argument about suffering. The central existential claim that Christianity makes is that suffering, while intrinsically an evil thing, can be turned to spiritual good. Christ came not to reign as an earthly king and lead armies against His enemies. (He would leave that to Mohammed.) Instead, He came to lay down His life as reparation to His Father for the sin of Adam and the subsequent sins of every single human being to walk the earth. His anguish on the cross and the blood He spilled were the single perfect sin-offering—which He told us to re-enact in the form of the Eucharist, at which the priest stands in for Christ, presenting the perfect sacrifice to the Father for our benefit. The cross—the first-century equivalent of the electric chair—became an emblem Christians would venerate. What is more, Jesus told us that if we would follow Him, we would have to pick up our own crosses and carry them. In other words, our daily frustrations and pains—even the agonies suffered by Christian martyrs—were a means of uniting ourselves to Him. St. Paul said that we must "make up what is lacking in the sufferings of Christ" by spiritually uniting our own sufferings to His.

This is heady stuff, and it can sound pretty off-putting. Some early Christians misinterpreted it and thought they had the duty of seeking out martyrdom. They would turn themselves in to the Romans who persecuted the Church—more out of puzzlement than anything else— in order to get to heaven faster. The Church condemned this mistake, and over time it made clear that suffering is a tool we can use to get closer to God. We shouldn't seek out suffering—we weren't made that way—but when it comes, as it comes to all of us, if only in the form of frustration, we should put it to use. We should, essentially, recycle it.

Sometimes, you are suffering because, as the hedonists claim, you are doing something wrong. Perhaps you are in an abusive relationship, or you are trapped in a job you aren't called to be doing. Pain was intended by God as a warning light that something is going wrong. But much of the time, thanks to the Fall, we suffer even when we're doing something right. Think of what happens to women when they give birth or soldiers when they fight for their country. Whatever anguish, confusion, even simple boredom comes our way in the course of living out a virtue … that's what we need to recycle. And the Church tells us how: by thinking of Christ on the Cross, and uniting our sufferings to His. That simple act of psychological empathy with the Passion can turn otherwise futile misery into a powerful spiritual tool. It is also liberating, since it transforms whatever abuse we are suffering and can't avoid into a means of getting to heaven faster—or helping others get there by praying for them.

It is this method of harnessing suffering and turning it on its head that has made life bearable and meaningful for poor and oppressed people all through history—and that kept the inmates of political prisons, from Alexander Solzhenitsyn to St. Maximilian Kolbe, from simply committing suicide. In our own, much nicer lives, we can keep this method in mind whenever we are tempted to take the easy way out, and shrug off doing the right thing in favor of the cozy thing. Instead of feeling degraded by whatever we are going through, by drawing closer to the suffering Christ, we are in fact being elevated. That's what the great St. Lawrence understood when the Romans were roasting him alive over a grill. So he told them, "I am done on this side, you may turn me over." And the Church made him the patron saint of chefs.

That explains the Christian attitude toward suffering better than any essay.

John Zmirak is author, most recently, of The Bad Catholic's Guide to the Seven Deadly Sins *and the graphic novel* The Grand Inquisitor. *He is the editor of* Disorientation, *and his full biography appears at the end of this book.*

Recommended Reading:

√ *Alcoholics Anonymous (The Big Book)*, by Anonymous (New York: AA World Services, 2002).

√ *Enemies of Eros*, by Maggie Gallagher (Chicago: Bonus Books, 1989).

√ *A Grief Observed*, by C.S. Lewis (New York: HarperOne, 2001).

√ *Lost in the Cosmos: The Last Self-Help Book*, by Walker Percy (New York: Picador, 2000).

√ *A Severe Mercy*, by Sheldon Vanauken (New York: HarperOne, 1987).

sophomore Follies

"[C]hange is a development which abandons nothing en route,
which does not superannuate either Shakespeare, or Homer, or
the rock drawing of the Magdalenian draughtsmen."
– T.S. Eliot, "Tradition and the Individual Talent"

PROGRESSIVISM

Peter Kreeft

> Progressivism, or "chronological snobbery," confuses
> "new" with "true." It also confuses facts with values,
> by using a factual, chronological term to carry a value
> meaning. Hence, something "modern," "contemporary,"
> or "current" is "truer," "better," or "more reliable."

Though snobbery was once quite popular and even socially acceptable in Europe, it was never popular in America. But one form of it still is, in both continents: chronological snobbery. The only people it is still polite to be snobbish toward is our ancestors, those who can't talk back because they are dead. (Most people are, you know. We are the small and arrogant oligarchy of the lucky-to-be-living.)

A clever debater once accused William F. Buckley of having "one of the finest minds of the thirteenth century." Buckley replied, "I don't deserve that compliment." Buckley was not a progressivist; his debate partner was.

That debater was the kind of person who uses the term "medieval" to mean not only "the millennium between about 500 and 1500 A.D." but also "primitive, superstitious, and unenlightened." Indeed, the very term "Middle Ages" was coined by the progressivists of the so-called "Enlightenment" as a term of insult: the "Middle" Ages were in the middle between the two ages that were enlightened, namely pre-Christian paganism, especially the Greeks and Romans, and the new paganism of the post-Christian "Enlightenment." (Of course, from the Christian point of view, that period was in fact the great Endarkenment.) One polemicist called the Middle Ages "a thousand years without a bath."

The fallacy of Progressivism is peculiarly modern. In fact, as we have just seen, the typically modern use of that very word "modern" to carry a (positive) value judgment is part of the fallacy. But the fallacy goes back to the Book of Job, who detected it in his three "friends" and repelled it with the famous bit of sarcasm "No doubt you are the people and wisdom began with you!" It has also been called "the Whig theory of history," "The Idea of Automatic Progress," "Americanism" (by a papal encyclical, no less; see essay 12), and "Presentism." The term "chronological snobbery" comes from C.S. Lewis (to my mind the clearest and most useful Christian writer since Thomas Aquinas) in his autobiography *Surprised by Joy,* where he gives his friend Owen Barfield credit for inventing it.

Lewis defines and refutes it at once as

> the uncritical assumption that whatever has gone out of date is on that account discredited. You must find out why it went out of date. Was it ever refuted (and if so by whom, where, and how conclusively) or did it merely die away as fashions do? If the latter, this tells us nothing about its truth or falsehood. From seeing this, one passes to the realization that our own age is also "a period," and certainly has, like all periods, its own characteristic illusions. They are likeliest to lurk in those widespread assumptions which are so ingrained in the age that no one dares to attack or feels it necessary to defend them.[1]

Thus, chronological snobbery is the identification, or confusion, of "change" with "progress." "Progress" is a value-laden term: it means not just change but change in a certain direction, change for the better. It is like a graph in geometry that charts the movement of some entity (a business, a body's growth, a football player's "forward progress") not only horizontally, from past to future, but also vertically, from worse to better.

But the very notion of a "better" assumes a "best," a standard, a goal. And that standard has to be unchanging; for if the goal line itself changes, it is impossible to make progress toward it. Imagine a runner on first base trying to make progress toward second base while the second baseman is carrying second base with him into the outfield.

The typically modern mind is (1) skeptical of absolute, unchanging standards and (2) in love with the idea of progress. But this is a logical impossibility, a self-contradiction. Without an unchanging standard, there can be no progress, only change. To such people, "progress" means no more than "change," and therefore "change" means the same as "progress."

Only a people both jaded and bored by the past and the present, and also skeptical of any "vertical dimension," any absolute and unchanging standard, could possibly be so moved by the single word "change" that a presidential candidate could win an election by using that single word as his campaign slogan. Why not instead "rutabagas"?

The opposite of Progressivism is conservatism or traditionalism. A conservative, by definition, is a happy person, one who is happy with what is. It is only for that reason that he wants to conserve it. A progressivist, on the other hand, is by definition an unhappy person, one who is unhappy with what is. It is only for that reason that he wants to change it. A conservative is someone who thinks happiness consists first of all in enjoying the good things we already have. A progressive is one who sees happiness first of all in hoping to enjoy the things we do not yet have. Adam and Eve were conservatives until the Devil made them into progressives. For the Devil himself was the first progressivist. The other angels were happy with God and His will, but the Devil wanted to progress to something better.

In other words, progressivists try to tell truth with a clock instead of an argument. It is as silly as trying to tell time with a syllogism instead of a clock. Or a calendar, which is only a larger, longer clock. For to say that an idea is no longer believable simply because this is the twenty-first century, not the thirteenth, is no different from saying that an idea is no longer believable because it is now 11:00 p.m., not 10:00 a.m.

But even silly superstitions have reasons behind them, and these must be discovered, exposed, defined, stated fairly, and then refuted. And there are at some seemingly cogent reasons that people adopt Progressivism. False conclusions usually are deduced from at least partially true premises; otherwise they would not have the power to deceive us.

How Did We Learn to Think This Way?

One of the causes of chronological snobbery is a reaction to the opposite superstition, which often clouded the judgment of our ancestors: that "new" equals "false" and "true" equals "old." "New" used to be a word of suspicion and "old" a word of affection. Now, it is exactly the opposite. Modern children use the word "old" as an insult ("You old…!"). But the ancients used it as a compliment. Things used to be sold by pretending they were older than they are. (And this market for fake antiques still has some cachet for a small minority.) Now, things are sold by pretending they are newer than they are. "New" sells. This is especially true of *ideas*.

Both of these attitudes are prejudices, but the exposure of neither one is a justification of its opposite. Intellectual errors, like moral vices, usually come in pairs.

A second justification for Progressivism is the fact of evolution, which seems to apply to both the growth of the individual and the growth of the human race. As we grow, it *seems* we get smarter, bigger, stronger, and (in those senses) better, both individually and collectively.

Yes, but we don't get happier, or holier, or wiser. There are more, not fewer suicides (especially among young people) today than in recorded history; and nothing is a more telling index of unhappiness than that. We are not more saintly than our ancestors but more decadent. And we speak of "modern knowledge" but not "modern wisdom." In fact, we still speak of "ancient wisdom." There has been not a single Socrates, Plato, Aristotle, Augustine, or Aquinas for the last 750 years. Which is more important, wisdom or cleverness? Sanctity or power? Happiness or efficiency?

A third argument for Progressivism is the fact that there has indeed been progress—obvious, automatic, and spectacular progress—in one field: technology. And since this has both causes and effects in every other field, it seems reasonable to believe in progress there as well.

But it isn't. Cleverness in inventing machinery has no tendency to cause wisdom or virtue in the inventor. If anything, it causes pride, *hubris*, and addiction to the power the new machines give us. And that is regress rather than progress in wisdom and virtue and happiness. If "all power tends to corrupt," the same must be true of intellectual, scientific, and technological power. Why don't we make that inference? Might it be because the addict always lives in denial?

But (so goes a fourth argument) there seems to have been progress not just in the sciences but also in the humanities. *War and Peace* is better than *Beowulf* and Picasso is better than the Lascaux cave paintings, and Stravinsky is better than Gregorian chant.

The answer to that is very simple: No, they're not. Name one twentieth-century Homer, or Dante, or Shakespeare, or Rembrandt, or Beethoven. The humanities are an unmitigated disaster area today. Nine-tenths of our English departments are infected with deconstructionists and other radicals, who either reduce great works of art to "power relations" among "race, class, and gender," or else deny that art works have any independent meaning at all. *That* sort of infection does not respond to arguments, only to exorcists.

A fifth argument points to the virtue of hope. This is one of the three greatest things in the world, one of the three "theological virtues," along with faith and love. How can you have hope if you don't believe in progress? The two ideas seem almost identical.

But there are at least four differences. First, progress is faith in yourself, or in humanity, to pull itself up by its own bootstraps; hope is faith in God's grace. Second, the idea of progress means that long-range improvement is guaranteed; but hope, like faith, is a leap, not a guarantee. Third, progress is a collective idea, but hope is an individual virtue. Fourth, progress means something this-worldly, but hope's object is other-worldly. (Paradoxically, hope for heaven does have powerful consequences for this world too: throughout history, those who have contributed the most to the improvement of this world have always been those who had a lively hope for the next.)

What's Wrong with Loving Progress, Man?

Progressivism is a form of snobbery, and has the same terrible moral effects as any other form of snobbery. In fact, it is snobbery masked, and therefore is even more harmful than open snobbery. It is a form of pride, the deadliest of the deadly sins.

If, as Chesterton said, Tradition is the democracy of the dead, then Progressivism is the elitism of the living—and within that, of a certain educated, well-off subset which enjoys sneering at once at its ancestors and its neighbors. Progressivism stifles the voices of the past and amplifies the sound of our own speech, the better to help us pretend we have heard all points of view, then do exactly as we wish.

Progressivism also cuts us off from what tradition gives us: a pile of precious intellectual and cultural gifts from our ancestors. And even when we receive the gifts and use them, we are not grateful for them, for Progressivism forbids us the virtue of humility, which is necessary for the acceptance of gifts; and from gratitude, without which there is simply no wisdom or happiness. There is no surer hallmark of holiness, happiness, and health, in individuals or societies, than gratitude, and no surer hallmark of their opposites than ingratitude.

Progressivism stems from logical fallacies and leads, by habit, to the disparagement of reason. The substitution of calendars for arguments not only proceeds from irrationality but also fosters it.

Worst of all, Progressivism clearly contradicts the very idea of a divine revelation. If there is such a revelation, Progressivism corrects it, corrects God Himself, and arrogates to itself the right to edit rather than deliver the divine mail, evaluating it by dating its postmark. Even religions that do not claim a direct divine revelation, like Confucianism, Taoism, or Buddhism, get their teachings from their past, from their founders. Progressivists make it up as they go along.

The Causes of Chronological Snobbery

It is one thing to point out the arguments people offer to defend Progressivism, and another to identify the reasons—many of them irrational—that they actually stumble into this superstition. The former are typically rationalizations for the latter. The first cause of widespread Progressivism is a society-wide attention-deficit disorder (ADD), boredom with the "same old thing," and addiction to "change," which comes from contempt for the past, not hope for the future—as if progress was defined only by getting farther from zero rather than closer to infinity.

Unthinking love of change for the sake of change is also *easier.* It is passive. It puts less mileage on the brain's odometer than the active and critical demand to find out whether the change is for better or for worse. Simple "change" is one-dimensional and automatic. Embracing it means also conflating the easy and comforting idea of irresistible progress with the difficult virtue of hope, which requires a constant active effort of each one of us.

There is also a religious—or rather, anti-religious—reason why our culture promotes Progressivism. Let me lay it out in the form of a syllogism (a very *old* and *traditional* form of reasoning):

a)   Since genuine progress necessarily implies a fixed, unchanging goal that does not change, and

b)   this is what religion claims to give us, therefore

c)   a secular state fears that this connection, however indirect, will pollute politics and thrust us back into the period of religious wars, which was ended by the separation of church and state.

Does this sound exaggerated? Think about how often people who defend traditional values are accused of hearkening back to "the Middle Ages." Ask yourself how long in any argument about the Catholic Church does it take a progressivist to mention the Inquisition? It's worth timing this phenomenon on your watch.

There is also in modern man, despite his protestations of independence, individualism, and autonomy (or perhaps precisely *because* of this) a deep, unacknowledged desire for conformity to the Zeitgeist, "the spirit of the age," "what everybody knows." It is surprisingly difficult to think for yourself, but only those who try to do that know that.

This is actually a mild form of possession. For those who have become possessed by a demon, an evil spirit, an alien, *another* spirit than their own true self, have lost not only their own identity but even the knowledge that there is a distinction between themselves and their possessing spirit. They are so deeply self-deluded that they sincerely believe that the thoughts emanating from their mind come from within, not from without. This is as true of possession by the Zeitgeist as it is of possession by a demon.

What's the Antidote?

To destroy the superstition of Progressivism, we must restore reason to its proper place, as an insight into truth rather than a rationalization of our desires or ideologies. We must correct defective theories of knowledge such as rationalism, empiricism, and idealism— offering answers from the annals of sound philosophical reasoning, e.g., Aristotle and St. Thomas. We should answer honest skeptics such as Freud by critiquing their arguments logically; if he treats (as he does) all reasoning as a rationalization for unconscious desires, we must point out that this applies to his theories, too. We should ignore dishonest skeptics (see essay 9, "Cynicism") who only want to sneer and enjoy jerking our necks by their chains.

We must think vertically, about timeless truths, before we can think horizontally, about timely, changing things. For without an appeal to some knowledge, however implicit, of a higher, unchanging reality, we cannot judge or improve anything real in this changing world. We must overcome our *aeternophobia*, our fear of eternal things. (There are new mental diseases in the modern world, just as there are new physical ones.)

We must moderate our fear of fanaticism. While we should never behave fanatically, Our Lord calls on us throughout the gospels to adopt a total, fanatical, uncompromising honesty with Truth—no matter what the cost. We must especially devote ourselves to the truth about the two persons we can never escape in time or in eternity:

ourselves and God. The finally important question is whether those two persons will spend eternity together, or apart.

We must educate ourselves about our past, our ancestors, our tradition, and our history. (And by "our" I mean the universally human, not only our local subgroup, whether nation, race, class, ideology, religion, or sex.) To generate the indispensable virtue of gratitude, we must know the riches that we should be grateful for.

To judge any change as progressive or regressive, we must eventually ask ourselves the Big Question: what is our final end, goal, purpose, *summum bonum* or greatest good. We must ask nothing less than the question of "the meaning of life," however unfashionable that question has become. If we don't have a clear vision of the ultimate finish line, we can't even know whether we are running toward it or away from it.

But to perform these cures one more thing is necessary. Even if the patient has received the perfect diagnosis, prognosis, and prescription, he will not recover if he will not take his medicine. The *will* is the key that starts the car of the psyche. "The readiness is all." If we do not *will* it, it will not happen. Wishing, dreaming, longing, and thinking, even the clearest and most rational thinking, will not move our feet one inch.

There always comes a time, after thinking and inquiring and writing and reading, to put those things away—not because they are mere toys, or because they are dispensable (they are indispensable!) but because they are means to a greater end. They are maps, and maps are means for moving, for marching. An army of map collectors will win no battles.

So let us march.

Peter Kreeft (Ph.D., Fordham, 1965) is, in order of importance, a Roman Catholic, married with four children and five grandchildren, professor of philosophy at Boston College, and the author of sixty-five books. His website is www.peterkreeft.com.

Recommended Reading

√ *The Everlasting Man,* by G.K. Chesterton (San Francisco: Ignatius Press, 1993).

√ *Surprised By Joy: The Shape of My Early Life,* by C.S. Lewis (Boston: Houghton Mifflin Harcourt, 1995).

√ *Those Terrible Middle Ages: Debunking the Myths*, by Regine Pernoud and Anne Englund Nash (San Francisco: Ignatius Press: 2000).

√ *The Essential Russell Kirk,* by Russell Kirk (Wilmington, DE: Intercollegiate Studies Institute Books, 2006).

√ *The Thirteenth, Greatest of Centuries,* by James Joseph Walsh (Nabu Press, 2010).

Notes

1   C.S. Lewis, *Surprised by Joy* (New York: Harvest Books, 1955), 207-8.

"Who is the Tolstoy of the Zulus? The Proust of the Papuans? I'd be glad to read him."
– Saul Bellow, novelist

MULTICULTURALISM

Robert Spencer

> **Multiculturalism is an anti-Western ideology that urges us to view the achievements of Judaeo-Christian civilization with a jaundiced eye and to overlook the flaws in other civilizations, in order to redress the results of past injustices. It is the intellectual equivalent of affirmative action quotas.**

In asking about the Papuan Proust, novelist Saul Bellow summed up the core problem with the twin idols of our age, Multiculturalism and diversity. For the ideology of Multiculturalism—now dominant on most college campuses—posits as a dictum that there *is* a Tolstoy of the Zulus, and a Proust of the Papuans, and that it is only white racism and Western Judeo-Christian chauvinism that has prevented these unheralded geniuses from receiving their due recognition.

And so high school and university textbooks now feature these putative literary lights cheek-by-jowl with Shakespeare, Dickens, and Faulkner, and if anyone dares point out that the nonwhite, non-Christian literary emperors are naked indeed, the charges of "bigotry" and "racism" will rain down.

After Strange Gods

And literature is the least of it. The hegemony of the multiculturalist idea is universal and complete. Today, no one questions the idea that one culture is as good as another. No one even whispers the possibility that the achievements of one group in a given area (for instance, medieval Christians) might actually surpass those of another group. No one even dares to think that there might be better indicators of the quality of an endeavor than the number of different ethnicities of the people involved.

Multiculturalism is one of the most successful heresies in history: it is as dominant in America and Western Europe today as Calvinism ever was in Geneva, or Anglicanism in Elizabethan London. Multiculturalism is the entrenched ruling dogma of the United States of America. The victory of the multiculturalist idea is so complete that those in thrall to its dogma do not even seem to notice the grotesqueries in which it involves them.

On November 5, 2009, Army Major Nidal Hasan opened fire at Fort Hood in Texas, murdering thirteen people and wounding thirty others. A flood of details quickly emerged that established not only that Hasan was an America-hating Islamic jihadist, but that his Army superiors had known this for several years and yet continued promoting him out of fear that if they did not do so, they would offend against the multiculturalist ethos that prevails in the U.S. military and society at large.[1]

And it's true: if anyone had reported Hasan, American Muslim advocacy groups would have immediately risen up in protest, and the mainstream media would have carried worried "exposés" about "bigotry" in the U.S. Armed Forces. The person who filed the report would have faced nationwide scorn and ridicule, and maybe even disciplinary action. No one who sins against the gods of Multiculturalism and diversity can expect to get off lightly. And so even General George Casey, the U.S. Army chief of staff, paid homage to these reigning idols when, just days after the massacre, he worried about the possibility of "a backlash against some of our Muslim soldiers"—which never materialized—and declared: "Our diversity, not only in our Army, but in our country, is a strength. And as horrific as this tragedy was, if our diversity becomes a casualty, I think that's worse."

Excuse me? The loss of "diversity" is worse than the wanton

murder of thirteen people? We really are dealing with a new religion here, one willing to sacrifice innocents to its gods. Casey's appalling comment marked the apotheosis of the multiculturalist ethic, heralding its absolute triumph in American public life.

Biting the Hand that Feeds You

And yet, for all its unparalleled and unquestioned ascendance, Multiculturalism is a heresy—one that can, like all heresies, bamboozle the unwary, dazzling them with the partial truths it contains. Since all human beings are creatures of the one God, to value the contributions of various ethnicities may seem to be an extension of the idea of the dignity of the human person. The Church is catholic, universal, and so to deny the virtue of ethnic diversity may appear to manifest a dangerous parochialism, or even worse, a flirtation with the "idolatry of race and blood" against which Pope Pius XI thundered in his anti-Nazi encyclical *Mit Brennender Sorge* ("With Burning Anxiety").

And, indeed, it is the Catholic Church, more than any other world religion, which most fully embraces the real diversity of the human race—bringing the Gospel to all nations, and seeking (even more effectively after Vatican II) to "inculturate" her central tenets in the existing civilization of a people, rather than demanding that they accept the Western cultural "package" in which the Church's teachings may have arrived. While the process of sorting out what is essential and inessential can get messy (the Church in Africa, for instance, must struggle against the residual, pagan practice of polygamy), the Church works earnestly only to transmit the truths essential to salvation. And she is uniquely qualified to do so. Regardless of his culture, she teaches that

> [M]an will always yearn to know, at least in an obscure way, what is the meaning of his life, of his activity, of his death. The very presence of the Church recalls these problems to his mind. But only God, Who created man to His own image and ransomed him from sin, provides the most adequate answer to the questions, and this He does through what He has revealed in Christ His Son, Who became man. Whoever follows after Christ, the

perfect man, becomes himself more of a man. For by His incarnation the Father's Word assumed, and sanctified through His cross and resurrection, the whole of man, body and soul, and through that totality the whole of nature created by God for man's use.

Thanks to this belief, the Church can anchor the dignity of human nature against all tides of opinion, for example those which undervalue the human body or idolize it. By no human law can the personal dignity and liberty of man be so aptly safeguarded as by the Gospel of Christ which has been entrusted to the Church. For this Gospel announces and proclaims the freedom of the sons of God, and repudiates all the bondage which ultimately results from sin. (8) (cf. Rom. 8:14-17); it has a sacred reverence for the dignity of conscience and its freedom of choice, constantly advises that all human talents be employed in God's service and men's, and, finally, commends all to the charity of all (cf. Matt. 22:39).[2]

Multiculturalism might sound almost catholic in the abstract, like merely an avowal of ethnic diversity as a positive good and an effort to highlight the cultural and other achievements of people of differing backgrounds. But its partisans almost never take notice of the human dignity or cultural achievements of Christian, and particularly Catholic, Americans and Europeans. Multiculturalism in practice maintains that *all cultures are equal, but some are more equal than others.* And the cultures that invariably get the short end of the stick are those that are most fully steeped in Catholic values. Listen closely to the moralistic language your professors use when they talk about Western "colonialism" and "imperialism," and compare it to the neutral, even positive rhetoric they employ when discussing (for instance) the Islamic conquest and forced conversion of the Middle East, or other non-Western powers (such as the Mongols) that have engaged in aggression. Likewise, compare their heavy-handed condemnations of "sexism" in the West with their kid-gloves treatment of (or virtual silence about) sexual slavery and female genital mutilation in Islamic countries, female infanticide in India, or footbinding in China.

None of this is an accident. Rather, these are manifestation of the fact that Multiculturalism in reality is an anti-Christian, anti-Catholic, anti-Western exercise in moral and cultural Relativism (see essay 2). A true multiculturalist hates all forms of Christianity and Judeo-Christian civilization, but retains particular contempt and bile for manifestations of Catholic piety and culture. That is why liberal journalists will, on the one hand, defend the free speech rights of those who savage the papacy and the Church, while deploring the "insensitivity" of (for instance) the Danish cartoonists whose lives came under threat for gently lampooning Mohammed.

Open Borders and Dead Souls

Dutch parliamentarian Geert Wilders, one of the world's foremost victims of the multiculturalist anti-Western bias, noted this glaring inconsistency in a speech he had slated to give in London—before multiculturalists barred him from Britain for his opposition to Islamic supremacism and Muslim immigration. And Wilders traced it to its cause: "The differences between Saudi Arabia and Jordan on one hand and Holland and Britain are blurring. Europe is now on the fast track of becoming Eurabia." Wilders explained that this was "apparently the price we have to pay for the project of mass immigration, and the multicultural project." Mass Muslim immigration into formerly Catholic Europe, of course, is based upon the multiculturalist dogma that a "diverse" population makes for a stronger society than one dominated by a single ethnicity.

The practical effect of this idea is the leveling of all distinctions and the establishment of a thoroughly relativist society. Europe for the last thirty years has followed a consistent policy of admitting large numbers of immigrants from Muslim countries, and—because of the multiculturalist imperative—doing nothing to compel them or help them to become Europeans, with European values and European outlooks.

And why not? Why should enervated, multiculturalist, post-Catholic Europeans "impose their values" upon the Muslim immigrants? Only the most benighted, backward chauvinist, they say, would assume that his value system had any greater worth than that of the next guy. But that only holds true if the next guy is a Muslim, and the one refraining from imposing his values is a Christian Westerner. The multiculturalist obligation does not fall upon everyone equally. A Muslim immigrant to a Catholic European country is under no obligation to change his beliefs or behavior to conform to Christian or European sensibilities. To expect him to do so would be to transgress against the cardinal multicultural principle of "diversity" as the highest good. The same does not hold true of a Christian who moves to Saudi Arabia (where Bibles and crucifixes are simply illegal).

Paradoxical as it may be, however, this relativist anti-Christianity and anti-Westernism only serves ultimately to aid in the establishment and entrenchment of a belief system that is anything but diverse or tolerant. For all over Europe, Muslim immigrants, under the benign eye of the multiculturalist establishment, have set up ethnic/religious enclaves in which Islamic law and culture are respected, and the law of the land and its mores are not. What's more, these immigrants are in countries all across Europe becoming increasingly assertive about the applicability of Islamic laws to non-Muslims. For example, Islamic law forbids insulting Allah or Muhammad on pain of death. And while no serious Catholic should support the ridiculing of any religious figure, freedom of speech—especially speech that is insulting or inconvenient—has been generally recognized in the West as a key bulwark against tyranny and an important concomitant of the God-given dignity of the human person.[3]

Even now, European multiculturalists, working willingly in tandem with Islamic supremacists, favor restrictions on speech that is deemed to give offense (to a protected multiculturist ethnic group, that is, not to the dominant Judeo-Christian culture) or to be "hateful." Accordingly, blasphemy laws are being revived in several European countries, not because of a rebirth of Christian piety, but due to a multiculturalist will to avoid offending a non-Western, non-Christian culture. Proof of this assertion is the fact that these laws are *never* applied to *anti-Christian speech*—only to speech offensive to others (especially Muslims). Wilders, who is currently facing prosecution for just such offenses, explained in his abortive London speech that "the dearest of our many freedoms is under attack. In Europe, freedom of speech is no longer a given. What we once considered a natural component of our existence is now something we again have to fight for. That is what is at stake."

Professors and Double Standards

This contempt for Western values that are rooted in the Christian and Catholic tradition also manifests itself in double standards. Multiculturalist feminists, as I mentioned earlier, rail against the alleged oppression of Christian women in America while excusing far worse conditions among non-Christians. One case study (out of thousands) comes courtesy of Dr. Laura Briggs, associate professor of women's studies and head of the department of women's studies at the University of Arizona. Briggs recently gave an address welcoming new Ph.D. students to the department. In the course of this address, Briggs, author of *Reproducing Empire: Race, Sex, Science, and U.S. Imperialism in Puerto Rico*, praised the work of other professors, including that of Saba Mahmood, associate professor of social cultural anthropology at the University of California at Berkeley. Mahmood, said Briggs, "confronted one of the legacies of a long history of orientalism and the recent wars in the Middle East: the way we are invited to see Muslim women as hopelessly, painfully oppressed, without their own autonomy, will, or individual rights."[4]

So apparently the rampant and systemic oppression of Muslim women—the veiling, seclusion, divinely-sanctioned beatings (disobedient women are to be beaten, according to Koran 4:34), the devaluation of inheritance rights and testimony, polygamy, and all the rest—has nothing to do with Islamic law or culture; it is merely a by-product of "orientalism and the recent wars in the Middle East"—in other words, it is the West's fault. This is Multiculturalism in its purest form.

"If we sometimes notice other Middle Eastern women—women's rights activists, for example," Briggs continued, "it is only to reinforce the notion that the great mass of Muslim women are terribly oppressed by the rise of conservative religiosity, by their husbands, by the ways they are compelled to dress."

Briggs had good news: Saba Mahmood, she said, spent two years in

Egypt and discovered that such oppression is just a mirage: "But after two years of fieldwork in the women's mosque movement in Egypt, Mahmood asks us to consider a new question: what if community, as much as or more than the notions of individual rights, is a route to living meaningfully? Perhaps we ought to rethink the idea that women's agency and personhood spring from resistance to subjection, and attend to the ways that in conservative religious communities, the cultivation of virtue and of closeness to God, of certain emotions and of forms of embodiment, are challenging but hardly one-dimensional ways of producing the self."

Once one hacks through the pseudo-intellectual, multiculturalist gobbledygook, it becomes clear that Briggs was essentially saying that if women felt fulfilled in being subjugated as inferiors under Sharia law, their good feelings were more important than their oppression and subjection, and rendered that oppression of no concern. And therein lies the double standard: one wonders what Betty Friedan or Gloria Steinem might have said in the 1960s if this same argument-from-fulfillment had been posed to them regarding American Christian women (see essay 10, "Feminism").

And aside from being inconsistent with what had been the feminist view of Western women's alleged oppression, Briggs's welcoming attitude toward the oppression of Muslim women—*as long as they're happy*—represented a betrayal of those women, whose suffering is objective, ongoing, and largely unnoticed. But feminists like Briggs never gave Christian women who were happy as housewives the same kind of respectful deference.

The underlying reason for that is that Multiculturalism, in the final analysis, is not really about respecting all cultures equally at all. The very idea of that is manifestly absurd, in any case—as if Nazi Germany and ancient Athens, or human-sacrificing Aztec Mexico and Catholic Spain, were essentially moral equivalents. But while it is true that thinking seriously about this core multiculturalist principle immediately lands on in the quicksand of Relativism, that Relativism is not in itself the ultimately focus or goal of the multiculturalist initiative. Since Multiculturalism was fashioned in the hard-Left groves of post-Sixties academe as a stick to use to beat the West, and particularly the Church, why *shouldn't* feminists coo over the forced and feigned happiness of oppressed Muslim women while insisting that perfectly happy Christian women are actually miserable? Denigrating and ultimately destroying the Judeo-Christian West, not stamping out some putative racist devaluation of other cultures, is the point of the whole multiculturalist enterprise.

And once that goal is accomplished, if it is accomplished, Multiculturalism itself will be swept away. It will have served its purpose. And in its place there will be established a tyranny far more severe and hateful than anything the multiculturalists themselves ever ascribed to bad old Catholic Europe.

Robert Spencer is the director of Jihad Watch, a project of the David Horowitz Freedom Center, and is the author of ten books on Islam, jihad, and related issues, including the New York Times *bestsellers* The Politically Incorrect Guide to Islam (and the Crusades) *and* The Truth About Muhammad, *as well as* Inside Islam: A Guide for Catholics. *His website is* www.jihadwatch.org.

Recommended Reading

√ *On The Immorality of Illegal Immigration*, by Rev. Patrick Bascio, C.S.Sp.,
   (Bloomington, IN: AuthorHouse, 2009).

√ *The Immigration Mystique*, by Chilton Williamson Jr. (New York: Basic
   Books, 1996).

√ *The Making of Europe*, by Christopher Dawson (Washington, DC:
   Catholic University of America Press, 2002).

√ *The Politically Incorrect Guide to Western Civilization*, by Anthony M.
   Esolen (Washington, DC: Regnery Publishing, 2008).

√ *The Camp of the Saints*, by Jean Raspail (Petoskey, MI: The Social Contract
   Press, 1994).

Notes

[1] For ample documentation of this sad fact, visit *www.jihadwatch.org* and
     read the articles tagged "Fort Hood."

[2] Second Vatican Council, *Gaudium et Spes*, no. 41.

[3] For more on the Church's support for liberty, see Avery Cardinal
     Dulles, S.J., "Enjoying and Making Use of a Responsible Freedom,"
     www.acton.org/publications/randl/rl_article_396.php.

[4] For all the details and documentation, see my article "Feminists
     Betray Muslim Women," *Frontpage* Magazine, May 21, 2009,
     http://97.74.65.51/readArticle.aspx?ARTID=34946.

"[Anti-Catholicism] is the deepest-held bias in the history of the American people."
– Arthur Schlesinger, Jr., historian

Anti-Catholicism

Jimmy Akin

> **Anti-Catholicism, as used in this essay, is the belief on the part of other Christians that the Catholic Church has a false gospel, is a force for evil in this world, or (as some say) the "Whore of Babylon" leading people away from the true, "biblical" form of the Christian faith.**

*Y*ou're sitting in your dorm with your laptop, trying to make the most important decision of the day: Facebook, Warcraft, or Faulkner? Playing WoW would feel too much like obvious goofing off. At least Facebook you can justify as keeping in touch with "friends." That essay on Light in August *can wait. You look over a bunch of friend requests from goofballs you haven't seen since high school.*

Then your roommate, a real live friend, comes back, and he has brought you a latte. Cool. "Hey, thanks!"

He straddles a chair and gives you one of his high-beam smiles.

"Dude, I'm going to the Bible study at the Interdenominational Student Center on Wednesday night. Do you want to come along? There will be girls."

You kind of knew that your roommate went to those things, but this is the first time he has tried to get you to go. You don't say anything.

"It's just a bunch of people getting together to study the Bible. I'd really appreciate it if you came with me."

"I don't know ..." you say. But eventually he wins you over, and you agree to go.

Wednesday night rolls around. At the Bible study, your roommate shows you around, and when he introduces you to a particularly nice-looking girl, she asks, "So where do you fellowship?"

"Um ... you mean, what church do I go to?"

"Right."

"Oh. Well, I go to St. Charles Borromeo."

She looks kind of puzzled. "So you're a Catholic."

"Yeah," you say uncertainly, not sure what to make of her reaction.

"We just love having Catholics here!" she says quickly.

"We sure do!" your roommate adds. "We love everybody!"

"We just want everyone to know Jesus Christ," the girl says. "Do you? Have you accepted Jesus Christ as your personal Lord and Savior?"

Losing Your Religion

If something like that hasn't happened to you, chances are good that it will. Many Catholic college students are invited to go to Bible studies, fellowship meetings, youth nights, hiking and camping trips, or worship services sponsored by non-Catholic churches and organizations. These groups often bill themselves as "interdenominational" or "non-denominational," meaning that they are open in principle to people from all Christian traditions. In practice, however, they almost always have a distinctly Protestant slant and—frequently—an anti-Catholic slant, as well.

Anti-Catholicism is a problem that dates back centuries. When the Protestant Reformation occurred five hundred years ago, feelings ran very high. Literal wars were fought. And while the Christian churches get along much better today, Anti-Catholicism still exists.

As its name suggests, Anti-Catholicism is hostility toward the Catholic faith. This is not the same as simply disagreeing with Catholic teaching. Virtually all non-Catholics disagree with one or more Catholic teachings—otherwise they would join the Church. But some go beyond disagreeing with the Church and actually view it as a force for evil in the world.

They may not own up to this. Did you notice how the people at the Bible study stressed how they loved Catholics? This is a common tactic, and it is based on a tricky use of language. What anti-Catholics mean when they say that they "love Catholics" is something like, "We love Catholics! We love them so much we want them to become *real* Christians instead." Some anti-Catholics view the Catholic Church as evil, believing that it has a "false gospel" that will lead people to hell. Some even say that it is the Whore of Babylon from the book of Revelation or that the pope is the Antichrist.

And yet they profess to love Catholics. There is a sense in which they do. But their concern for the salvation of individual Catholics doesn't change their hostility toward the Church and its teachings. They really do think it is evil.

The fact that Anti-Catholicism often tries to mask itself, to hide its hostility to the Church, makes it a particular threat. It is easy to get caught up in a round of fun social and religious activities with a group of people who seem friendly and open. It can be easy to make friends with them—or even date them—and have them get involved in your life, only to have a rude awakening when you realize that they have been teaching you things contrary to the Catholic faith or that they are trying to get you to leave the Church.

Look at what happened to the Catholic student in our story. His new roommate turned out to be one of these people. What's going to happen next? He may have to endure the fellow's Anti-Catholicism (now that it has started to come out into the open) or find somewhere else to live. What's worse, he might not know his Catholic faith that well—or might not know that there are answers to the arguments his new friends will put to him. He might start buying into their arguments and even leave the Church.

Fortunately, there are answers to the claims made by anti-Catholics, and we are going to look at some of them. First, though, we need to note something: anti-Catholic Christians are often committed, zealous, and courageous in preaching and living their faith. They are sincere Christians who may have engaging worship services with dynamic preaching, powerful music, and emotional, heartfelt prayer. And they can give a sense of tight, close-knit community. Those are good things, but they can be found in *all* Christian communities—

which only shows us something else: *None* of these positive aspects are tests of what is *true*. We need to recognize what is good in any movement—Anti-Catholicism included—but we ultimately must look at what is *true*, since "the Truth will set you free" (John 8:32).

Taking Scripture Literally

Many anti-Catholics say that the Bible should be interpreted literally. But even the staunchest literalists recognize that *some* things in Scripture are symbolic, for instance when Jesus calls His disciples salt (Matthew 5:13). The question is: *Which* things are symbolic and *which* aren't? By saying the Bible should be taken literally, anti-Catholics generally mean something like, "If a passage *can* be taken literally, it *should* be taken literally."

This creates a pro-literal *bias* that doesn't do justice to the ancient authors. To see how, let's take an example from today. Suppose some people learn that an important dignitary is going to visit them. One might say, "We better roll out the red carpet." You and I, as English-speakers, know that this is a figure of speech. There isn't really (or isn't *usually*) a red carpet that gets rolled out. Now suppose someone is new to English and hasn't heard this phrase before. If he uses the rule proposed by anti-Catholics (if something *can* be taken literally then it *should* be), he will misunderstand what is being said.

Red carpets *are* sometimes rolled out—at the Oscars, for example. But usually they aren't. People familiar with the phrase know this. So the proper question isn't, "*Can* this phrase be taken literally?" but "*What* do English-speakers mean when they use it?"

We should apply the same principle when reading Scripture—not asking, "*Can* this passage be taken literally?" but, "*What* did the ancient writers *mean* by their different forms of expression?" We must be careful and thoughtful as we read, recognizing that they had a sophisticated culture that appreciated poetry and symbolism.

An even more important problem with the anti-Catholic way of using the Bible is the idea that we should learn about God from Scripture *alone*. This "Bible only" view is often used to challenge opposing viewpoints. Frequently, it comes in the form of the question, "Where is *that* in the Bible?" This supposes that the thing in question *should be* found in the Bible and, if it's not, it's illegitimate.

Where does this assumption come from? It is not something that the Bible actually teaches … and that is a problem. If we are supposed to get our teachings from the Scripture alone then we *need* to get the "Bible-only" teaching from Scripture alone. And we can't.

There are passages anti-Catholics appeal to, but a careful reading shows that *none* says what anti-Catholics need them to say. For example, in Mark 7, Jesus criticizes the Pharisees for ignoring the teachings of Scripture on the grounds of their tradition. He contrasts the word of God with the "traditions of men." From this, many anti-Catholics conclude that anything not found in the Bible must be a "tradition of men." But this doesn't follow at all. God communicates His word in various ways, and the written form—Scripture—is only one of them (see Isaiah 55:10-11, Luke 3:2-3, John 1:1, Acts 4:31, Romans 2:14-15, Hebrews 11:3).

Tradition is not automatically a bad thing. Tradition is simply what is "handed down" (this is what the word literally means), and *everything* handed down from Christ and the apostles is important, whether handed down in written form or not. In 2 Thessalonians 2:15, Paul says to "stand firm and hold to the traditions which you were taught by us, either by word of mouth or by letter."

The New Testament has quite a number of positive things to say about tradition (see 1 Corinthians 11:2, 2 Thessalonians 3:6, 2 Timothy 2:2)—which is so disturbing to those who hold the "Bible-only" view that some Protestant translations (e.g., the New International Version) use the word "tradition" whenever it is spoken of negatively but "teaching" whenever it is spoken of positively—even though the original Greek term is literally translated as "tradition."

How Can I Be Saved?

Remember the question that the Bible study girl asked the Catholic student in our story: Had he accepted Jesus Christ as his personal Lord and Savior? This kind of question is often at the heart of the anti-Catholic's concern. If you answer, "I sure have!" then the anti-Catholic likely will conclude that you are a true Christian. If you don't quickly and confidently say yes, however, then you need to be evangelized and "get saved."

The problem is that the "accept Jesus as your personal Lord and Savior" language is not found in the Bible. On the day of Pentecost, Peter did not get up and say, "Men of Jerusalem, accept Jesus as your personal Lord and Savior!" (Look at Acts 2:38-39 to see what he actually said.) Nor did Paul say this anywhere in his travels—or in his letters. This language actually arose in American Protestantism. It is a kind of jargon whose meaning is obvious to those use it but foreign to everyone else.

It is no surprise, then, that most Catholics are startled by the question and don't really know what to say when they are asked it. This language is not from the Bible, and it is not the kind of language used in the Catholic community. The fact that Catholics don't use this language does not mean that they haven't responded properly to the Gospel or that they aren't "saved" (i.e., in a state of grace). It just means that they use different language.

Not By Faith Alone

Sometimes anti-Catholics use other questions, like, "Have you invited Jesus into your heart?" (More jargon; not found in the Bible.) In any extended discussion of salvation, there is one phrase that is virtually guaranteed to come up. This is because anti-Catholics, like Protestant Christians generally, hold that we are saved "by faith alone."

Different groups interpret this in different ways, but for anti-Catholics it often means something like this: To be saved, I must place my faith in Jesus Christ as Lord and Savior, and at that point all my sins are forgiven—past, present, and future—and I can never lose my salvation. Nothing else is needed, neither baptism nor other sacraments. At most, those are mere symbols. If I were to see them as having any role in salvation, they would be "good works," which Paul says are *not* what justify us.

This view has a number of problems.

Scripture nowhere says that we are saved by faith alone. In fact, the only time that this phrase appears (in James 2:24), it is *rejected*. James tells his readers: "You see that a man is justified by works and *not by faith alone*" (emphasis added). Anti-Catholics have their own ways of interpreting this, but they are on dangerous ground if their signature phrase—"by faith alone"—is rejected the one place it is used. Certainly, this is not the language that Scripture uses to describe our salvation.

If one looks at what Scripture does say is needed to be saved, different passages stress different things, but it comes down to three: repentance from sin, faith in Christ, and new life through baptism (Mark 1:15, John 3:5, 3:16, Acts 2:38, 22:16, Romans 2:4, 6:3-4, 1 Peter 3:21).

What about the idea that all our sins are forgiven—past, present, and future—so that we can never lose salvation? This is hard to reconcile with the words of the Our Father, in which Jesus told us to pray, "Forgive us our debts, as we forgive our debtors" (literal translation). This is the model Christian prayer, and it implies we have an ongoing need for forgiveness. Of course, we were forgiven all our past sins when we became Christians, but if we commit new ones, we need new forgiveness.

The idea is also hard to square with passages in the New Testament that warn about falling away from grace (see Luke 8:13, John 15:1-6, Romans 11:20-24, 1 Corinthians 15:2, Galatians 5:4). Fortunately, if we do commit mortal sin and lose our salvation, it is possible for us to come back and be forgiven. That's the *point* of the parable of the Prodigal Son (Luke 15:11-32). The younger son starts out as a genuine son of the father, then leaves for a life of sin. His father describes him as "dead" and "lost," but he repents and is welcomed by the father, who describes him as "found" and "alive again." So one can have spiritual life, lose it, and regain it. How does this happen? Ordinarily, through the sacrament of reconciliation (confession), which is also firmly grounded in Scripture (John 20:21-23).

What about good works? There has been a huge misunderstanding on this point. It is very true that you don't have to do good works—meaning, good actions inspired by the supernatural love of God—to enter a state of salvation. In fact, you can't. God doesn't pour supernatural love (charity) into our hearts until He saves us. Good works *flow from* being in a state of salvation, and God rewards them in various ways. Paul says that God "will render to every man according to his works: to those who by patience in well-doing [literally, "working good"] seek for glory and honor and immortality, he will give eternal life" (Romans 2:6-7; see also Galatians 6:6-10).

It may surprise anti-Catholics, but Paul does not have a negative attitude toward good works. *Whenever* he mentions them, he says positive things. So what are the works he rejects? "Works of the law." But the law Paul is talking about is the *Torah*, the Law of Moses (Genesis through Deuteronomy). That is why, *whenever* he rejects "works" as a means of salvation, he associates them with being a Jew and observing circumcision or the Mosaic food laws or Jewish feast days. What he is fighting is the idea that one must be an observant Jew to be saved—as some people in the first century thought (see Acts 15, Galatians 1-2).

Paul's message is that we aren't saved by doing the works prescribed by the Mosaic Law. Instead, both Jews and Gentiles are saved through Christ and—once in that state of salvation—we are to do good works (see Ephesians 2:8-16). This is also why baptism and the other Christian sacraments aren't "works of the law." They can't be, because the Law of Moses doesn't require them!

Interacting with Anti-Catholics

Even if *they* don't view you as a Christian, anti-Catholics *are* fellow Christians. They are fellow believers in Jesus Christ. Anti-Catholics have good and bad points, and we must recognize both. As Paul says, "test everything and hold fast to that which is good" (1 Thessalonians 5:21). Agree where we can agree; disagree amicably where we can't. Discussions with them can turn poisonous, so *make sure you don't add any poison*. Speak the truth in love (Ephesians 4:15), and "avoid disputing about words, which does no good, but only ruins the hearers" (2 Timothy 2:14). If we disagree, make sure we are disagreeing about substance, not terminology or matters of emphasis.

Be aware also that there are many Protestant Christians who *aren't* anti-Catholic. They may have inherited some of the ideas and language we talked about above, but they may still view the Catholic Church as truly Christian and as a force for good in the world. This view has grown in recent years, in part due to the pro-life movement, as well as greater dialogue between Protestants and Catholics.

A special kind of anti-Catholic you may meet is the ex-Catholic.

People who leave the Church and join anti-Catholic groups are often given a kind of grid through which to view their prior life as Catholics. They are taught to say things like, "The Catholic Church never taught me about Jesus—or my need for grace, et cetera."

A good response to this kind of claim is, "Really? When you went to Mass, didn't you say the Creed, which talks extensively about Jesus and His life, death, and resurrection? Didn't you say things like 'Lord, have mercy' and 'Lord, I am not worthy to receive You,' signaling your need for grace? The Church was so concerned that you understand these things, it wrote them into Mass itself. Was the problem that you weren't really paying attention? Maybe you should take a more sympathetic look at the Catholic Church."

Whatever way the discussion goes, stick to one subject at a time. It is a natural temptation, if you are unsure what to say, to change the subject. Don't indulge this. Don't pepper each other with charges so that the other can't respond properly. And if you don't know the answer, say you will check it out. If you aren't in the habit of reading the Bible—the world's most Catholic book—then this is the perfect time to start.

Jimmy Akin is senior apologist at Catholic Answers (www.catholic.com). He blogs at jimmyakin.org and at ncregister.com. His books include The Salvation Controversy, The Nightmare World of Jack Chick, The Fathers Know Best, *and* Mass Revision—*each published by Catholic Answers.*

Recommended Reading

√ *Born Anti-Catholic, Born Again Catholic,* by David Currie (San Francisco: Ignatius Press, 1996).

√ *Catholicism and Fundamentalism,* by Karl Keating (San Francisco: Ignatius Press, 1988).

√ *Surprised by Truth,* edited by Patrick Madrid (Dallas: Basilica Press, 1994).

√ *Crossing the Tiber,* by Steve Ray (San Francisco: Ignatius Press, 1997).

√ *By What Authority?* by Mark Shea (Huntington, IN: Our Sunday Visitor, 1996).

Junior Delusions

"Just as G.K. Chesterton ... once argued "pragmatism doesn't work," it
might be said that utilitarianism doesn't have utility. How does a society
maintain moral order in the face of a standard relying on expediency?"
– Herbert London, college dean, professor, president of the Hudson Institute

UTILITARIANISM

Dwight Longenecker

> **Utilitarianism is the ethical theory that pleasure is the greatest good, suffering the greatest evil. Therefore, our actions must be guided by calculating what will bring the most pleasure or least suffering to the largest number, regardless of other considerations.**

I love my iPhone. I want it to work. I want my laptop not just to work, but to work every day in a whiz-bang way. I want it quick. I want it reliable. I want it smooth. I want the useful things in my life to be dependable. I want the trash collected on Thursdays and the mail delivered every day. I want my flights to come and go on time, and I want my luggage on the carousel when I land. I want to set the air conditioning at the temperature I choose. I want the electric, the cable, the gas, and the phones all to work. In other words, I want to utilize the utilities, and in that sense, like everyone else I am a (small "u") utilitarian.

But that's where my Utilitarianism ends. To understand why my Utilitarianism ends there, I first have to explain where it begins—and before I explain where it begins I had better explain what it is.

Utilitarianism is a very simple philosophy that believes not in good works, but that what works is good. In other words: if something does the job, if it is efficient, if solves a problem, then it is good. In fact, this philosophy is so simple that it could be the philosophy of beasts. It is a sort of animalistic instinctive response:

- "I am hungry, so eating is good."
- "I am frightened, so I must flee or fight."
- "I desire pleasure, so pleasure is good."

Apply this primitive logic to governing the whole of one's life or human society, and what you have Utilitarianism, which has been summed up as "the greatest pleasure for the greatest number of people." The hedonist (see essay 3) might say, "If it feels good, do it," but the utilitarian corrects him: "If it feels good *for most people*, do it." Therefore, in a society that derives pleasure from efficiency and economy, it is concluded that the effective and most economical solution is always the best one.

The Roots of the Rot

Utilitarianism was first propounded by the eccentric Englishman Jeremy Bentham (1748–1832). His most famous ethical maxims are: "The greatest good for the greatest number," and "Pain and pleasure are the sovereign masters governing man's conduct." Bentham's ideas were expounded and expanded by the philosopher John Stuart Mill (1806–1873). However, as with most concepts in philosophy, Bentham's and Mill's Utilitarianism is the outgrowth of a previous train of thought, namely, the writings of the Scottish philosopher David Hume (1711–1776). Hume was an empiricist. Trusting only in the knowledge gained from human reason and the sensations of the physical world, he was skeptical about the spiritual aspect of existence, especially the miraculous. Bentham accepted Hume's disbelief in anything other than this physical realm, and drew conclusions that seemed to make sense: If there is nothing but this world—no afterlife, no heaven or hell or final judgment—then let us build a paradise on earth. Furthermore, let us build that paradise quickly, for building a paradise is long, hard work and we haven't much time before our final oblivion.

These ideas may sound unfamiliar, and I have dropped a lot of names, but what would you think if I told you that most people in

America are deeply influenced by Utilitarianism? Indeed, many self-proclaimed Christians have become utilitarians by default because of two assumptions that lurk unexamined at the foundation of modern culture.

The first one is democratism. In its pure form, democratic theory assumes that the majority doesn't just rule—it determines what is right and wrong. Every time you hear a journalist or politician refer to a position as "mainstream" (as opposed to "fringe") he is arguing from this principle: that truth comes not from reason or revelation but from *consensus*. It is a tiny skip from this to the conclusion that whatever pleases the majority must be morally right—even if that means legalizing practices such as abortion.

The second assumption is Scientism (see essay 11), which has conditioned our culture to believe that truth can only be found through experiments that can be quantified.

Therefore, if it can be *calculated* that something gives many people pleasure, this is evidence that it is moral. In our market economy, people vote with their pocketbooks, so when a large number of consumers "vote" for something (be it peanut brittle or pornography), we have democratic, scientific evidence that it is right.

The Problems with the Pleasure Principle

Let's see how this principle works in practice, and the paradoxes it can produce. When a toddler is screaming it seems obvious that his mother could make the child happy by giving him a lollipop. The problem is that too many lollipops rot a baby's teeth, and he soon has more pain than pleasure. Furthermore, by rewarding his screaming, a mother may be spoiling her baby and producing an adult who will never be happy unless he has a constant supply of pleasures. So Mother may decide that in the long run it would be better (and more pleasurable) for baby to not receive his lollipop, to learn self control through self-denial and become a better and therefore happier person.

This simple illustration reveals the underlying problems with the utilitarian pleasure principle. There are four basic problems, which I like to call the *Four P's*:

1. *Personal Taste.* One man's pleasure is another man's pain. I

like grand operas. You like soap operas. I like hot dogs. You like hors d'oeuvres. The baby likes yelling and lollipops. The mother likes silence and self-discipline. Who is to say which pleasure is more pleasant? If this is true of individuals, who is to say what really brings pleasure to the greatest number of people? Would it be possible to construct some sort of scale of pleasures? Would base physical pleasures be "lower" while intellectual pleasures would be "higher"? Who would make these judgments? How would they do so? Why should their decisions be final? Wouldn't they simply reflect the personal tastes of those in power?

2.   *Proportionality.* Shall we judge on pleasure alone, and if so, how do we judge what is most pleasant? Do we judge by the *intensity* of the pleasure, the *duration* of the pleasure, or simply by the *number* of people who are pleased? The quality and the quantity of both the pleasure and the pleased is impossible to assess. Is a mild, long-lasting pleasure better than a sublime, but fleeting one? Are the pleasures of the masses really more important than the pleasures of the elite? Shall we cater to the high falutin' or the *hoi polloi*? If we are seeking the greatest pleasure for the greatest number, then we must decide for the base vulgarities, not the exquisite but rare experience. But are the crude pleasures truly better than the sublime? Surely not. Suddenly, the simple calculus of pleasure proves far more complex than we first imagined.

3.   *Pain.* Ironically, the pursuit of pleasure invariably brings pain, and there is a universal wisdom that the greatest pleasures actually involve the greatest pains. I must practice for years and sacrifice many opportunities for enjoyment if I wish to play Rachmaninov's Third Piano Concerto. If I desire the exhilarating pleasure of standing on the top of Mount Everest, I must first go through the exhausting pain of climbing the mountain. Even athletic excellence requires intense exertion; as the phrase goes, "No pain, no gain." This seems to be how we are built, but it confronts the utilitarian with a mystery:

that pleasure and pain are always mixed, and you cannot have one without the other any more than you can have light without shadow.

4. *Power.* As the example of the mother and the toddler shows, we don't always know best how to maximize our long-term pleasure. This is also true of adults—who will overeat and refuse to exercise, gamble away their life savings, smoke cigarettes, and expect society to fund their cancer treatments. Since we know that many people will fail to "max out" their lifetime supply of pleasure, shouldn't those who know better intervene to impose on them wiser choices? Shouldn't the government serve as a kind of a Ministry of Pleasure, hiring scientists and bureaucrats to research what will offer most of us maximum happiness, then pressuring us to make the right decisions? If "the greatest pleasure for the greatest number" is the guiding principle, then this principle overrides any concern for individual autonomy and gives the people in power license to dictate all our choices. If this seems to you far-fetched, think for a second how strange your grandparents would have found it that in some parts of our country gay "marriage" is permitted, but smoking is virtually prohibited; prayer in schools is forbidden, but seat-belts are mandatory. What was it that turned things (from their perspective) upside down? Utilitarianism in power. What happens when its power grows? How much freedom will any individual retain?

The Consequences of Consequentialism

Utilitarianism is sometimes called *consequentialism* because the morality of an action is based on its outcome. This raises the question, "What are the consequences of consequentialism?" It might be a simple equation to say that what is good is what brings the most pleasure to the most people, but it doesn't require much thought to see that consequentialism is actually self-defeating. The utilitarian cuts off the branch he is sitting on.

Because of the four problems of Utilitarianism (Personal Taste, Proportionality, Pain, and Power), seeking the most pleasure for the most people will instead bring about large-scale suffering, perhaps even slavery.

This conclusion is inescapable. In the absence of any criteria for deciding what is truly pleasurable, Utilitarianism can only work if some Authority, somewhere, *decides* what brings the most pleasure. It must decide how much of that benefit is desirable. As a side effect of introducing that pleasure, the authorities must inflict some pain—either the pain of self-discipline to obtain the pleasure, or the pain of "pleasure" imposed on people who do not want it. ("You will sit through this diversity training session and *like* it.") Finally, the authorities must impose the pleasure using forceful means of some sort. Since the only ethical standard is long-term pleasure for the many, there will be no moral restraints on how that power is exercised. Efficiency, even ruthlessness, can be justified if they serve the goal.

Utilitarianism starts as an instinct, develops into a theory, and then grows into a method. Pursued consistently, it becomes a utopian ideology. Utopianism is the misguided ambition that one can build a paradise on earth—and history has shown that such a fantasy always leads to tyranny. For a utopia to be created, the old, existing order must be overthrown. As Lenin said, "You cannot make an omelet without breaking some eggs." (By "eggs" he really meant "heads.") Such revolutionaries may have the dream of bringing about the greatest good for the greatest number, but the means they are willing to use include totalitarianism and torture. The civilian death toll for utopian ideologies in the twentieth century—from Hitler's "Thousand-Year Reich" to the Communist "workers' paradises" that once covered half the planet—has never been fully calculated, but it well approaches 170 million.[1] (See essay 13, "Marxism")

Once Utilitarianism morphs into utopianism and the revolution is accomplished, the people whose pleasure is allegedly the goal are never pleased for very long. The members of this new society have very high hopes, and since our disappointment is directly proportional to our expectations, when paradise doesn't pan out, their bitterness increases exponentially. How awful it is when their brave rebellion's leader turns into a ruthless tyrant, when the revolutionaries prove more corrupt and cruel than the king they overthrew! What misery for the masses when their dream is dashed and the paradise is controlled by a politburo.

Granny Must Go

"Okay," some might say, "Utilitarianism may be poison in politics, but what about in our personal lives? If we restrict this theory to individual decisions, surely what brings happiness for the largest number of people must be right." When Granny is in a nursing home, having lost her marbles, and lies in bed drooling all day, what shall we say? Granny has no real quality of life. She demands constant care. Constant care is expensive. Is it not more merciful (and cheaper) to simply assist her to her final journey home? She will die soon anyway. Is it not better for all the rest of the family, indeed for all the rest of society for Granny to go?

When utilitarian solutions are applied at the personal level, we feel in our bones the ultimate cruelty of this philosophy. More chillingly, the utilitarian does not regard himself as being cruel. According to his lights, he is being kind—and doing so more efficiently. In seeking the greatest good for a greater number, he judges each of his actions *quantitatively*. For him, what is large is always better than what is small. A large group of people is worth more than any individual, as a flock of ninety-nine sheep is much more important than the single one who wanders off lost (see Matthew 18:12–14; Luke 15:3–7).

There is just one fatal flaw in the utilitarian's arithmetic: Every group, herd, or flock is made up of *individuals*. A man with no respect for the individual will have no real respect for a group, since zero times ninety-nine still comes out to zero.

The utilitarian has no use for the individual because his ideology is built on a foundation of materialism. He does not mind euthanizing Granny because he does not think she possesses that precious, invisible treasure—the human soul. Indeed, the utilitarian is constantly tempted to disbelieve in the reality of any realm other than the material world of sensations. The consistent utilitarian will kill because he does not believe in an afterlife. He is sending his victims to oblivion. Eliminating them is no worse than putting cats to sleep or pulling weeds. Furthermore, since there is no afterlife, the utilitarian also has no fear about his own destiny. When his time comes he too will simply cease to exist. That being the case, he will never have to answer for his crimes, and if there is no system of justice, can we really even call them crimes? At worst, they might be called miscalculations. As Josef Stalin once said, "A single death is a tragedy; a million deaths is a statistic."

If There is No God, Everything is Permissible

Because utilitarianism is rooted in materialism it also slides toward atheism. If there is nothing but the material world of sensation, how can God exist? Where is there any room for an objective moral law? Therefore, Utilitarianism must also be relativistic (see essay 2). Instead, "good" is what *seems* most pleasurable for the most people at any given time. Of course, this perception can change—which is why utilitarian ideologies come in so many different colors, packages, and flavors, and frequently are found at war with one another.

It cannot be otherwise, since Utilitarianism, like every form of Relativism, denies that there is any such thing as truth. But if there is no truth, then why should the pleasure principle itself be true? It might be just as true that what is good is what brings pleasure to only a certain group of people, or to only one person (for instance, myself). For that matter, it might just as well be argued that bringing pain to millions is good. Without a sound basis for what is true or false, anything (or nothing) could be true.

Therefore, we must conclude that the proposition, "What is good is what brings the most pleasure to the most people" cannot be true. The utilitarian might reply that it may not be eternally true, but at it does make more people happy so it is good. But goodness and truth are two sides of the same coin, and if a thing is not true, then it is not good either. If there is no such thing as truth, then there can be no real test for goodness. The utilitarian is above all a practical man, so at this point he will wave his hand at such philosophical nit-picking and say, "Well, it may not be true or good philosophically, but at least it is a practical program for human happiness, and that is the best we can hope for." But as we have seen, the pleasure principle is impractical, impossible, and leads both to tyranny and misery. It is therefore not even true to its own inner principles.

Climbing Off the Squirrel Wheel

Just because it isn't consistent or true, that doesn't mean Utilitarianism isn't influential. Most of us have been affected to one degree or another by the thoughtless Utilitarianism that pervades our secular culture. An easy, materialist, pleasure-loving ethos drives much of what we do as capitalistic, democracy-loving Westerners (see essay 8, "Consumerism"). Do we not, most often, act according to "the bottom line"? In our own quest for pleasure, do we not make moral choices based on ease, economy and efficiency alone?

What is the alternative? Instead of the easy Utilitarianism that teaches that "what works is good and true," we need to re-examine an ancient idea common to the great philosophers (Plato and Aristotle) and the saints: "What is good and true works." In other words, we must pursue the Good for its own sake, and we will find as a side-effect that we are happier. Some pain will be involved, since nothing good in a fallen world comes easily. In our search for what is really Good, we will ask what is really True, and that must lead us to consider what is really Beautiful. If that three-part statement makes you think of the Blessed Trinity, you are already on the right track.

Rev. Dwight Longenecker attended Bob Jones University, then Oxford University, where he trained to be an Anglican minister. He is now parish priest of Our Lady of the Rosary Parish in Greenville, South Carolina. He also serves as Chaplain to St Joseph's Catholic School. He is the author of a dozen books, including The Gargoyle Code, *and many articles in the Catholic press. He blogs at "Standing on My Head."*

Recommended Reading

√ *Aliens in America: The Strange Truth About Our Souls,* by Peter
  Augustine Lawler (Wilmington, DE: Intercollegiate Studies Institute Books,
  2002).

√ *Introduction to Philosophy,* by Jacques Maritain (Lanham, MD: Sheed and
  Ward, 1944).

√ *The Four Cardinal Virtues,* by Josef Pieper (Notre Dame, IN: University of
  Notre Dame Press, 1966).

√ *A Guide for the Perplexed,* by E.F. Schumacher (New York: Harper
  Perennial, 1978).

√ *Ideas Have Consequences,* by Richard M. Weaver (Chicago: University of
  Chicago Press, 1984).

Notes

[1] Scholar R.J. Rummel, in his book *Death by Government* (New Brunswick,
     NJ: Transaction Publishers, 1994), estimates the total number of
     civilians intentionally killed by government action in the twentieth
     century at 169,198,000. The vast majority of these were killed by utopian
     regimes motivated by some variety of Utilitarianism.

"True happiness flows from the possession of wisdom and
virtue and not from the possession of external goods."
– Aristotle

CON$UMERI$M

Eric Brende

> **Consumerism is the contemporary face of avarice,
> which drives individuals to define themselves
> and judge their value in terms of material
> acquisition and the social status that it confers.**

O nce upon a time, nobody wanted to be called a heretic. The designation brought with it shame, social opprobrium, and, in some cases, imprisonment, exile, torture, or even death.

Those days are long past. Now the charge of heresy is actively sought. A heretic, especially if so named by official representatives of the Church, may look forward to fame, glory, and possibly wealth. Bishops rarely denounce members of their own flock who flout them, for fear of actually *aiding* a heretic's cause. To be an openly, articulate gay or "pro-choice" Catholic is to garner invitations to TV talk shows, glowing book reviews in the *New York Times*, and general public favor. To dissent from the Church is to ascend in the world.

But the new norm has its exceptions. One of these, undoubtedly, is the little-mentioned heresy of Consumerism. No one speaks openly in favor of rabid, acquisitive behavior. The mark of Consumerism is a stain from which Church, state, and media all equally recoil, for the most part. Of course, it has never been considered Christian to gorge oneself on food or material things. Nor is it now politically correct. It doesn't even accord with FDA recommendations on diet.

Even the Amish Catch It

That doesn't keep everyone and his uncle from falling rapturously into Consumerism's arms. Consumerism is the national open secret. Its capital "C" is the scarlet letter everybody wears under the lapel or purse flap. In our hearts we know our passion for things is un-virtuous, un-ecological, un-hip. (Precisely, in part, because it may expand the hips).

The waddling sway of Consumerism is so magnetic, not even the last, most intransigent holdouts can resist its spell. I speak of the Amish.

The Amish were never ones for fashion, nor for materialistic self-indulgence. In the popular imagination, they remain icons of frugal, thrifty living. My knowledge of these (former) ascetics comes first-hand: I lived and worked among them for several years. And it is true that a core set of Old Order stalwarts still does, in fact, live a duly Spartan existence.

But visit Lancaster County, Pennsylvania, the heartland of these latter-day Puritans, and the veil falls from your eyes. Don't listen to what the tour guides tell you about Amish bans on telephones, electricity, and cars. Take a good look for yourself. Behind the old homestead, just outside the kitchen door, you will see phone booths. Listen, and you may hear what sounds like a fire alarm going off— that's the phone ringer, set so loud you can hear it from indoors. There, in the inner haven of Amish tranquility, modern appliances have been rigged to run on pressurized air fed in through wall outlets hooked up to gasoline-driven pumps.

See that van whoosh by? Look closer and you will spy a group of men in long beards and black hats—suspiciously Amish-looking— driven by their paid chauffeur in a leased Suburban, perhaps on their way to a Phillies game, where they may well own a private box. Other bearded, black-hatted men will not be visible at all because they are wintering in Florida at the Amish condominium community known as Pinecraft, near Sarasota. Not wanting to fall behind the times, Amish today carry cell phones, run websites, and ching-ching at electric cash registers.

But don't tell the Amish they are no longer Amish! No indeed. For one thing, that would be bad for business. "Amish" is now a brand name. Simplicity is a major sales angle. Simplicity is *hip*. Every week in *Parade* magazine, two-page ads run picturing an Amish carpenter alongside the "wood-burning" electric fireplaces he is hawking. On every Midwestern interstate, billboards tout Amish-made furniture, food, and amusements. Odd how a horse-and-buggy society thrives on car commerce.

So why spend any time considering such a peculiar group as the Amish?

Our Culture's Dirty Secret

The Amish story is the American story writ small. Culturally, we descend from a religious group no less ascetic than they—namely, the Puritans. Later followed waves of immigrants, including many Catholics, whose core values, in turn, derived from the sacrifices of disciplined Benedictine monks. But would anyone casting a glance over our society today be able to guess our origins? Somehow, over time, both Amish and mainstream Americans have traded a life centered on frugality and hard work for one of engorgement and sedentary entertainment. It is just that the Amish have been somewhat slower to succumb.

Still and all … it may be difficult for any of us to admit we are *bona fide* consumerists. We may, on the contrary, work hard all day and try to spend as little money as possible. And that just shows how sneaky the germ of Consumerism really is: even after we've come down with a full-blown case of affluence, we still feel deprived!

Richer Than King Tut

To put our true condition in perspective, we need some concrete measurements. According to hard-core environmentalist Bill McKibben, every American child enters the world toting a Macy's Day Parade-sized balloon of incipient needs and wants behind him. Is this fair? How accurate is McKibben? Consider these facts:

- It has been calculated that the average American consumer (the word now effectively has replaced "citizen") continually relies on an amount of motor power equivalent to *the efforts of 200 horses or 1,200 human slaves laboring night and day.*

- In terms of sheer monetary wealth, the average American consumer spends *in a single day* what the average Somalian does *in three months*.

- Our combined possessions, if strung out end to end like Christmas tree lights, would *stretch to the moon and back*. King Tut would have been envious.

But maybe not. If King Tut and his entourage had gone through as many plastic bags, cardboard, newspapers, clothing, rusty old washing machines, refrigerators, sofas, side tables, rugs, and other disposables as we do, his slaves would have been too busy constructing pyramid-sized landfills to have any time to build his tomb. This is not to mention that mechanical horses discharge a more noxious flatulence than biological ones and would have engulfed sunny ancient Egypt in a shroud of smog. And if Tut had had to buy gasoline, he might have become beholden to the nomads of neighboring Saudi Arabia sooner than we have. Also, Tut might have died sooner from obesity and clogged arteries.

Now we begin to see the shame of Consumerism. We glimpse how each of us can be richer than an Egyptian Pharaoh and claim that we're still downtrodden. We start to understand why we don't admit to our card-carrying Church of Consumerism membership: Consumerism is *embarrassing*. Consumerism brings blatant costs. Stuff is not weightless, dimensionless, or maintenance-free. Being stuffed, medically, is unhealthy and expensive to treat. And all material things and technological playthings cost money up front, which we pay for on credit or by working longer hours, separated from our fellow men, women, and family members in various corporate or educational cubicles.

Chaining Ourselves to the Shopping Cart

The deepest and most insidious aspect of Consumerism, nonetheless, is something else altogether. It is non-material or psychological, an insidious dynamic of addiction. It has even been given a fearful, pseudo-technical name: the "hedonic escalator." This mechanism of deepening misery, which is nicely illuminated in Laura Rowley's book *Money and Happiness*, works by a series of stages:

> *Step one.* We are introduced to a new amenity, technology, or comfort. We nibble.

> *Step two.* We nibble some more until it becomes part of our daily diet. We get used to it.

> *Step three.* We no longer feel the pleasure it first gave us, only pain when we go without it. This is the critical step. *Voila!* What was once a carefree want is now a crying need. The harmless trifle binds us like a chain.

While many of his philosophical ideas were highly questionable, Jean Jacques Rousseau was at his best when he made this declaration about the slavery of our belongings: "Being deprived of them became much more cruel than possessing them was sweet" and we were "unhappy about losing them without being happy about possessing them."[1]

Advanced-stage Consumerism might be thought of as something like anorexia, but in reverse. The anorexic looks in the mirror at her emaciated frame and sees only vestiges of fat. The terminal consumerist looks at his three-car garage with its SUV, BMW, riding lawn mower, mountain bikes, weed whacker, automatic door opener, deluxe tool cabinet ... and sees only the missing leaf blower.

From Luxury to Heresy

But given all this, is Consumerism really a heresy? Isn't it, rather, a moral weakness, a vice?

Here, as elsewhere, heresy comes in only when we *justify* a sin, when we try to legitimize or downplay it and contort our belief system and way of life in the process (think of "liberal Catholic" dissent on Church teachings concerning sexuality). Instead of admitting to avarice, we *rationalize* it. And so we conceal, even from ourselves, our ravenous appetite for stuff. And at the same time we slyly subordinate the only true God to the god of the marketplace. We worship mammon. As we slip unwittingly into the unacknowledged heresy of Consumerism, we slowly begin to replace the cross of Christ with a golden calf.

First, we slyly substitute euphemisms and code words for the truth about what we are really up to. The ancient Christians were able to practice their faith in the midst of a hostile, pagan civilization using sign language and symbols only they understood, such as the picture of a fish. We have our own mutually agreed-upon code words referring to neo-pagan practices in the midst of a post-Christian civilization. When we look at how healthy the economy is, we don't see what is really important—for instance, how many fathers of families earn the "living wage" Pope Leo XIII taught that they are entitled to.[2] No, we nervously watch Wall Street's "consumer spending index," then worry when it dips. Indeed, when the U.S. Government sent out "stimulus" checks during the 2008 economic crisis, one worry the Feds expressed was that people might save the money instead of spending it—as they were supposed to. Instead of scaling back on consumption as world resources dwindle, we spearhead the search for alternative energy—enabling us to consume as much or more than ever—and call ourselves "green," as if we had entered into a full-fledged love-embrace with Mother Nature. But we are only finding more and better ways to consume, with less guilt.

The Root of the Rot

Next, we may begin to connect our rationalizations to a system of thought long in subtle conflict with Christianity. First nurtured in the West by Sir Francis Bacon, it culminated in the brazenly materialistic ideologies of Adam Smith and Karl Marx. Seemingly opposed to each other, both "free market" and "Communist" schemes nonetheless aim to gratify an unending expansion of wants—Smith's in practice merely being more effective and less restrictive. Like William F. Buckley and his fellow neo-conservatives, we may then give more credence to "St. Adam Smith" than to the Pope. Finally, so busy producing and consuming and "amusing ourselves to death" (as Neil Postman put it in his classic book of that title), we treat our weekly stint at church as merely one perfunctory stop at another display case in the greater marketplace of life. I can remember a time when

Sunday really seemed like a special day. Most stores were closed and Sunday afternoon was a time for a leisurely family get-together. Now, a typical American Catholic shops and even works on Sunday, and at all events will be found basking in the glow of football broadcasts or home DVDs, whose special effects seem ever so much more dazzling than any modest miracles performed by Jesus in some old book.

Through it all, Consumerism still works mostly unspokenly. Nobody professes it during the time allotted for reciting the Creed. But the logic of it is written on our hearts just the same, and we see it in how we live our lives and express our priorities. Recall how Jesus met a wealthy young man who truly desired to follow Him but shrank back because he couldn't give up his possessions. "It is easier for a camel to go through the eye of a needle," the Lord lamented, "than for a rich man to go to heaven" (see Matthew 19:23-24; Mark 10:24-25; and Luke 18:24-25).

Clearly, the rich young man did not become rich to avoid a higher calling. Rather, his belongings had gradually encumbered him without his realizing it and, like an overburdened pack animal, he had forfeited the agility necessary to do what he really wanted. Emerson, centuries later, may have echoed Christ when he said: "Things are in the saddle and ride mankind."[3] Indeed, they ride us away from where our better selves would go.

The Way Out is the Way Up

But how can we get out from under that saddle? Overcoming attachment to material things calls for the opposing virtue of detachment, a kind of physical extrication, a relinquishment of dependency. We are all ensnared not only in our desires but in a system based on them and the upside-down priorities they represent. These priorities can drive us to reject even the gift of new, unborn life. According to the (pro-abortion) Allan Guttmacher Institute, twenty-seven percent of women who have abortions report that they did so for reasons centered on money, education, or career.[4] When it starts to have such lethal results, Consumerism really has become what John Paul II called a "structure of sin."[5] We all participate in a massive, interlocking economic machine churning out mountains of superfluous goods, and burying us in the process.

So we need more than a changed attitude; we need a detachment with teeth, a full-scale willingness to confront our situation, top to bottom. How do we obtain that? Fortunately, not all Amish have succumbed to Consumerism, and some still live a life reminiscent of the old Puritans and Catholic Benedictines. After visiting Lancaster, I stumbled upon one of these groups, lived among them for years, gleaned much about their secrets, and even wrote a book about them.

Among my bracing discoveries:

The *real* Amish have more time. Yes, they do all their physical work by hand or with horses. But there is more time at the end of the day. Compared to the rest of us, they are saturated by leisure.

The *real* Amish compress more of life into a given moment. This explains their leisure. Physical exercise, companionship, immersion in nature, contemplation—all are ingredients in a typical slice of Amish daily experience. This is because they work for subsistence (meeting their actual needs) instead of for luxuries (meeting self-made needs). I felt a wonderful, achy satisfaction at the end of a day working on an Amish farmstead. I had not been chasing trinkets and daydreams. I had been zeroing in on my true, bare-bones, human needs. There is no replacement for that kind of satisfaction.

The *real* Amish carry no burdensome debt. Most farmers borrow hugely to pay for giant tractors and enormous acreages in a cycle that forces them to get ever-bigger or get out, and in effect, consume more than they can afford. These farmers are always worrying. The *real* Amish, working small twenty- to fifty-acre plots for their own needs and a bit of extra cash, incur few debts and feel much freer.

The *real* Amish enjoy a certain, but limited, amount of material pleasure. Amish cooking is delectable. Amish farmsteads are beautiful. Amish families average eight (!) children. (The typical Amish family of nine or ten, however, leaves a smaller environmental footprint than the average American family with 2.1 children.)

The *real* Amish confer with each other to set limits on land, possessions, and technology. They pray together and make Sunday a genuine day of rest dedicated to God. By forging their destiny together, and putting God above everything, they, in effect, create a well-ordered, all-encompassing haven from the surrounding culture.

According to the Catholic vision of education, best summed up in John Henry Newman's *The Idea of a University*, a college campus is meant to serve as exactly that kind of haven. Temporarily exempt from Adam's charge to earn their bread by the sweat of their brows, students are called to spend those four short years engaged in the life of the mind for its own sake, in exploring their talents and expanding their minds, searching for the truth about man and his relationship to God. Along the way, they surely will pick up skills and specialties that will enable them to earn a living. But too many students—with the encouragement of parents and even professors—throw away this unique opportunity for soul-searching and learning for its own sake, and spend their college years either partying or prematurely yoking themselves to some specialization designed to prepare them for a career—all this before they have even really sampled the many areas of learning. We "settle" too soon, put on blinders, and look for the nearest pre-professional treadmill on which we can climb.

It is also worth supplementing the "liberal" arts with "practical" ones that give people more down-to-earth skills—of the sort that have been stigmatized ever since Aristotle as occupations worthy only of slaves. The Benedictines corrected that Classical misconception with the motto *ora et labora* ("pray and work"), showing that you could integrate the life of the mind with that of the body—by which I mean to say that there's no reason an educated person shouldn't consider plumbing or carpentry as a profession. At the very least, learning such practical arts will make you handier around the house.

Since Consumerism inverts every Christian priority, Christians can only respond by inverting Consumerism. Under Consumerism, material things rank highest, self-interest next, other people perhaps below that, and God last. In authentic Christianity, God comes first, others second, self third—and material needs last. Those healthier priorities should guide a students' choice of classes, extracurricular activities and even—I'll dare to suggest—of a career.

If each of us, individually, begins to invert our own priorities and gradually link arms with like-minded fellows, a new social order cannot fail some day to coalesce. The challenge is not so daunting as we think: for the more possessions we shed, the greater our moral agility, and the freer we will be to pursue, perhaps with a saucy swing of the hip, what God really wants of us.

Eric Brende is a graduate of Yale and the Massachusetts Institute of Technology (MIT). His book, Better Off: Flipping the Switch on Technology, *tells the story of a Catholic couple living among the Amish and is going on its twentieth printing.*

Recommended Reading

√ *The Shallows: What the Internet is Doing to Our Brains,* by Nicholas Carr (New York: W.W. Norton, 2010).

√ *In Defense of Food: An Eater's Manifesto,* by Michael Pollan (New York: Penguin, 2009).

√ *Giants in the Earth: A Saga of the Prairie,* by O. E. Rollvag (New York: Harper Perennial Modern Classics, 1999).

√ *CivilWarLand in Bad Decline,* by George Saunders (New York: Riverhead Books, 1997).

√ *Small is Beautiful: Economics As If People Mattered,* by E.F. Schumacher (New York: Harper and Row, 1975).

Notes

[1] Jean Jacques Rousseau, *Discourse on the Origin of Inequality*

[2] *Rerum Novarum,* no. 67

[3] "Ode, Inscribed to W. H. Channing."

[4] 2004 Alan Guttmacher Institute study, see *www.guttmacher.org/pubs/psrh/full/3711005.pdf.*

[5] *Evangelium Vitae,* no. 12

"The cynic knows the price of everything, and the value of nothing."
– Oscar Wilde, deathbed convert

CYNICISM

George William Rutler

> Cynicism is an intellectual stance that seeks to debunk
> the motives of other people and "expose" commonly
> treasured deals—generally for the sake of making
> the cynic feel superior to others, or freeing him
> from the necessity of attaining difficult virtues.

There was a time, and I was part of it, when college freshmen were required to learn venerable school songs before arriving to register for classes. Most of them had to do with the school's founding fathers, the superiority of its football team, the foibles of the faculty and, wistfully, elegies on campus sunsets. Then there was the Alma Mater.

Much, if not all, of that has been discarded, and I fear that rare is the college where the Alma Mater is not sung without some mockery, which is the cynic's way of burlesquing piety. The cynic, even a senior cynic, is always sophomoric. Piety is in his crosshairs because piety is reverence for one's ancestors, and the cynic has reverence for no one, especially for those who had greater hope than he for the possibility of attaining truth.

The Catholic scholars who formed the first great universities of Europe did so in the same age that popularized the image of the "Pieta" showing the Lady with Divine Wisdom on her lap. She reverences her own Son, whose divine Person existed before her. There is not much for students to sing about if they do not understand that.

Instead, learning divorced from reverence for knowledge makes school songs raucous, then rancid, and soon they fade away like an aftertaste of some remote harmony barely heard and rarely sung. This is similar to the awful silence, haunted and not holy, that saddened Shakespeare when the monasteries had been destroyed for being politically incorrect, and all the seasons were a withered autumn:

> *That time of year thou may'st in me behold*
> *When yellow leaves, or none, or few, do hang*
> *Upon those boughs which shake against the cold;*
> *Bare ruin'd choirs where late the sweet birds sang.* (Sonnet 73)

Political Correctness: Cynicism's Toxic Waste

Political correctness, by which I mean conformity to popular prejudice, has embedded itself in the schools which were meant to be engines of its refutation. The problem was well underway over a century ago when Chesterton wrote: "The more doubtful we are about whether we have any truth, the more certain we are (apparently) that we can teach it to children. The smaller our faith in doctrine, the larger our faith in doctors."

This had been the cynical mood of the utilitarians (see essay 7) in the nineteenth century, whose influence has pretty much dismantled the liberal arts and replaced them with job training. It is the inevitable corruption of the loftier minds known among the Greeks as the "cynics." These vagabond philosophers put no trust in the possibility of attaining higher knowledge, and found happiness only in living a simple ascetic life according to the norms of nature, pursuing the human virtues, turning their backs on money, entertainment, and even hygiene. Any college that places football over studies could learn from Crates of Thebes, who satirized the Olympics. As Cynicism found happiness in mastery over one's desires, it was prelude to Christ's command to seek first the kingdom and its righteousness and all else will be added.

The problem with Cynicism is that it had no Christ. To embrace Cynicism, the Emperor Julian renounced Christ. Yet he had studied with St. Basil the Great and St. Gregory Nazianzen in the same Athenian academy.

How Cynicism Eviscerated Catholic Colleges

In the 1960s, Catholic schools were swept up into an optimism about the future that no classical cynic would have fallen for, and soon that optimism—a thing very different from the virtue of hope—fizzled into disillusionment, frustration, and contempt for institutions, including the one instituted by Christ. Many schools were eager to distance themselves from the Church. This became a common Cynicism far different from the classical sort—which did believe in the goodness of the natural order and the possibility of happiness through virtue in benign harmony with nature. Instead, our schools have incubated a deep contempt for nature as the work of a Creator and for virtue itself. In 1967, presidents of Catholic universities held a grand conference at Land o' Lakes, Wisconsin. At its conclusion, they asserted that a Catholic university is "an independent organization serving Christian purposes but not subject to ecclesiastical-juridical control, censorship, or supervision." This statement betrays a very cynical assumption for a group of Catholic intellectuals—namely, that any structure and regulation outside itself is suspect and probably harmful. The assumption is that personal will and objective reason are enemies, and any authority other than the self is a censor of freedom. If that is true, then one must eventually also reject Jesus Christ, who "taught with authority and not as the scribes" (see Matthew 7:29; Mark 1:22).

Follow this thought to the logical extreme, and you reach a pure autonomy of the will, without reference to the logic of nature. Personal experience replaces historical experience and the classical concept of beauty as truth is replaced with Hedonism (see essay 3). While this is quite the reverse of cynical detachment, it flows from the cynic's materialist denial of transcendent truth.

Western Civ Has Got to Go

Personal "value" becomes the standard, even when it bears little or no relationship to virtue. Soon we slide into the pool of the merely subjective, like President Barack Obama's definition of sin: "being out of alignment with my values." This postmodernist diction cynically deconstructs logic and actually ridicules it—perhaps unwittingly because it has so absorbed the temper of illogic. And so the cynic threatens all social constructions built on values higher than the self, as when Rev. Jesse Jackson in 1988 led students at Stanford University chanting: "Hey, hey, ho, ho! Western culture's got to go!" (And it went: the school dismantled its once-admirable core curriculum.) Fragile acquaintance with that culture made the words easier to shout, and those who did shout were little aware that the culture they hated was all that secured their right to parade their ignorance. Blatantly, such attitudes tinge a Catholic school when it loses confidence in its own logic, and soon it retains its inspiration only as a vignette. It is not uncommon to see an institution describe itself, almost wistfully, as "in the Catholic tradition."'

The Wild Men of Athens

The classical cynic saw knowledge as tragic. This was an abuse of the Socratic idea of discontent. Socrates wanted a mind to be restless so that it might question and examine the self. This was the groundwork for scientific advancement and spiritual maturity, and St. Augustine developed it: "If you would attain to what you are not yet, you must always be displeased by what you are. For where you are pleased with yourself there you have remained. Keep adding, keep walking, keep advancing." This is very different from the parting blessing I once heard a university president bestow on a graduating class: "May you all find satisfaction." The ancient *cynici* believed in the virtues as the total reference for all living and knowing, to the extent of rejecting the worldly allurements of money, power, physical fitness, and celebrity—that is, all the gods of the modern university. So, by rejecting the virtues, modern Cynicism has become shabby burlesque of its ancient source. On the modern campus, it may be the fashion to be as disheveled as the extreme cynics who St. Augustine said "proclaimed their unclean and shameless opinion, worthy indeed of dogs." Take away the ancient regard for virtue, and the descent is straight and fast from the wild men of Athens to the wilder men of Haight-Ashbury.

And it was the latter who outgrew rebellion against their professors to become professors themselves, and who have already shaped a postmodern culture whose chief accomplishment has been the dismantling of virtue. One need not dress anymore like a Flower Child of the 1960s to exude their Cynicism. George Bernard Shaw did not dress like a hippie, but he did believe in words resonating in academic halls today: "The power of accurate observation is frequently called cynicism by those who don't have it."

The Cynicism of Pontius Pilate

Jesus had the most acute power of observation, but when He observed the lilies of the field (see Matthew 6:35), it was with a conclusion far different from that of Mr. Shaw. And when He spoke of truth to Pontius Pilate, He elicited a response as constrained as that of the proto-cynic, Antisthenes: "What is truth?" It is the same reaction you would get in a university today if a priest were to say he had a truth to proclaim. For the cynic has moved beyond disagreement about truth to denial that there is such a thing. Perhaps Pilate's question was sad. Today, it has become sarcastic. The voice in the lecture hall today says neither "You're right" or "You're wrong," but rather sighs, "Whatever." This is why it is difficult to engage honest debate in the academy today, for debate proposes a model of truth and defends it. Instead, the cynics developed a form of debate they called "Eristic" specifically for the purpose of confusing people, and causing onlookers to laugh at those who used real logic as mere religious fanatics. Does this tactic seem familiar? No doubt you have already encountered it on campus.

Classical Cynicism bred its eccentrics and Christianity bred its own: Diogenes wearing only a tub was perhaps no more neurotic than St. Simon Stylites, who prayed for thirty years on top of a pillar. But Antisthenes and Anthony of Egypt were equally eloquent against greed, and it was fashionable in recent years, by some fantastic stretch of imagination, for some biblical critics to intimate some influence of the cynics on Christ himself. But if the classical cynic, in misunderstanding Socratic discontent, saw the life of the mind in terms of insoluble tragedy, the modern cynic flees from that noble discontent by turning learning into therapy. "Feeling good about myself" replaces hard thinking and so, as classical Cynicism led to Stoicism, modern Cynicism leads to Hedonism.

Disdain for pleasure and intoxication by pleasure are two sides of the same coin. In that self-absorbed and self-satisfied universe, the university purveys fast and fleeting gratification, strokes people's conceits, limits their experience to that which is immediately accessible in popular culture, and subjects all judgments to a political egalitarianism that levels all distinctions of excellence, so that no art or achievement is superior to another.

Cynicism Leads to Hideous Campus Buildings

Anything more demanding on the reason and will is shunned and even mocked, as we see in the purposely ugly structures that have littered campuses since the 1960s, or the revenge of rock music on Bach, or the fashion of wearing shabby dress, like rich film stars appearing unshaven in expensive clothes. Even the minimal wearing of academic regalia on special occasions tends in such an environment to seem like an ironic pastiche.

The greatest victim of this self-conscious Cynicism is our liturgy itself, which is so often left devoid of beauty—and basically devoid of worship, since the cynic maintains only a cult of the self. When Cynicism invades, the academy becomes the nursery of the barbarism it was meant to defy and convert, and it is done with a supercilious sneer. When Belloc visited the ruins of the city Timgad in the solitude of the Sahara, watching the sand blow round the remnant Greek pillars, he wrote in a journal:

> We sit by and watch the barbarian. We tolerate him. In the long stretches of peace, we are not afraid. We are tickled by his irreverence, his comic inversion of our old certitudes and our fixed creeds refreshes us: we laugh.

> But as we laugh, we are watched by large and awful faces
> from beyond. And on these faces, there is no smile.

Thinking can engender Cynicism, but ultimately it endangers it. That great cynic Sir Francis Bacon once said, "Knowledge is power" (see essay 11, "Scientism"). But power itself is morally indifferent; only wisdom can render power pure. The ancient cynic disdained any identity of knowledge with power, and thought that power degraded knowledge, while the modern cynic substitutes power for knowledge. That Cynicism cancels free speech and prohibits any expression that contradicts the power of the day—so religion is the chief enemy.

Why did God forbid his first humans to eat the fruit of the tree of the knowledge of good and evil? It is not that he wanted them to be stupid. Quite the opposite: our first parents already had the gift of "preternatural" knowledge. God did not want them to become cynical. To partake of the knowledge of good and evil is to redefine reality: to say that up is down and in is out and good is evil and evil good. In *The Idea of a University,* John Henry Newman describes the kind of student produced by a culture of Cynicism:

> Mistaking animal spirits for vigour, and over-confident in their health, ignorant of what they can bear and how to manage themselves, they are immoderate and extravagant; and fall into sharp sickness. This is an emblem of their minds; at first they have no principles laid within them as a foundation for the intellect to build upon; they have no discriminating convictions, and no grasp of consequences. And therefore they talk at random, if they talk much, and cannot help being flippant, or what is emphatically called "young." They are merely dazzled by phenomena instead of perceiving things as they are.[1]

These "young" are perpetually adolescent, formed so by schools which themselves are culturally immature, narcissistic, and neglectful of their own moral sources. It should be no surprise that these institutions should then contradict their own claims to counter-cultural independence. The cynic, for example, will criticize the economic system which feeds him, living off endowments and grants and luxuriating in a system of privileged tenure which would have been the envy of a feudal lord. As classical Cynicism, wanting to upset convention, was a theatrical philosophy, needing an audience to make its point, likewise the modern university has sought to be popular rather than aristocratic in its disdain for received opinion—displaying pornography as art the way the Greek cynic Diogenes performed lewd acts in the marketplace, and insulting all authority save its own with a kind of constipated anarchism that tightly regulates its subversion of morals, absolute in the conviction that tradition is morbid and scandal is genius.

The Pope against the Cynics

I well remember a lecture in Cambridge University in 1988. I made the trip from Oxford, which a cynic might call one of the longest journeys in the world. The speaker illustrated the fatal attraction of philosophical relativism by recalling a visit to the widow of Ernst Bloch, an atheistic materialist. He told Mrs. Bloch that in the university today, the biggest problem was drug abuse. She covered her ears, because in this brave new world minds were supposed to have freed themselves from illusion by freeing themselves from religion, the opiate of the bourgeois masses. Although the weather that night was bleak, undergraduates stood out into the rain trying to hear this man who spoke on objective truth and the way philosophical relativism tyrannizes reason. This same thesis he would develop as the "dictatorship of relativism" when he became Pope Benedict XVI. The faculty of divinity seemed rather chill in their embrace of him, and a cynical newspaper account said that the interest of the students must mean that medievalism is the undergraduate fashion of the day.

Pope Benedict had hard experience of the way National Socialism, in its politicized Cynicism, once twisted language to accomplish its assault on reason. The more any system debases truth, the more it will debase language. If thinking is not important, then the ability to express thought declines, and so now we have widespread the remarkable inarticulateness of today's generation: "You know, you, know, I mean, like."

In his essay "Politics and the English Language," George Orwell had already seen the way this works: "A man may take to drink because he feels himself to be a failure, and then fail all the more completely because he drinks. It is rather the same thing that is happening to the English language. It becomes ugly and inaccurate because our thoughts are foolish, but the slovenliness of our language makes it easier for us to have foolish thoughts."

Orwell optimistically thought that the decay is reversible, that "to think clearly is a necessary first step toward political regeneration." By definition, however, regeneration is not the desire of the degenerate. A clarity of thought urged, for instance, by Pope Benedict is considered scandalous. Here is corroboration of Toynbee's thesis that civilizations die, not by invasion, but by suicide. Under the guise of sophistication, which is the cynic's borrowed fancy dress, the schools succumb to that self-destruction which they thought was self-improvement because they would not think beyond themselves.

In the eighteenth century, Giambattista Vico considered how civilizations move from barbarism to civility. Then comes a decadent period of "hyper civilization" in which the early strength that animated the best of civilization weakens and the arts of civilization reach a breaking point, like a singer struggling for a note beyond reach. The fourth stage is worse than a return to the first barbarism: it is a "barbarism of reflection" in which the new, inarticulate barbarians have no future—for they seek none, as they are deluded by the outward remnants of civilization, their technology and pleasures, into thinking that they are not barbaric at all. But that is the senile stuttering of a people for whom, as Edmund Burke said in his *Reflections on the Revolution in France*: "Vice lost half its evil by losing all its grossness."

Catholicism shaped the university by knowing the Creator of the universe, who gives civilization a "beauty ever ancient ever new." That is a classicism more permanent than timeless human perceptions because it comes from the Eternal God who makes "all things new." To make all things new is different from making all new things. There are a great many old things we should and must revere. So in a right Catholic spirit, songs should be sung in the schools, and certainly the

Alma Mater. But the student's best song is one that can be sung by old men, too, climbing the steps to the altar:

"Introibo ad altare Dei, ad Deum qui laetificat juventutem meam" – "I will go unto the altar of God, to God who gives joy to my youth" (Psalm 43:5).

Rev. George William Rutler is a priest of the Archdiocese of New York and pastor of the Church of Our Saviour in Manhattan. He is the author of many books, the most recent being Cloud of Witnesses *(Scepter Press).*

Recommended Reading

√ *In Defense of Philosophy,* by Josef Pieper (San Francisco: Ignatius Press, 1992).

√ *A History of Philosophy: Vol. I,* by Frederick Charles Copleston (Garden City, NY: Image Books, 1993).

√ *The Idea of a University,* by John Henry Newman (Notre Dame, IN: University of Notre Dame Press: 1990).

√ *The Oxford Dictionary of Philosophy,* by Simon Blackburn (New York: Oxford University Press, 2008).

√ *Philosophy 101 by Socrates: An Introduction to Philosophy Via Plato's Apology,* by Peter Kreeft (San Francisco: Ignatius Press, 2002).

Notes

[1]   John Henry Newman, *The Idea of a University,* Preface.

"*Feminism is doomed to failure because it is based on
an attempt to repeal and restructure human nature.*"
– Phyllis Schlafly, mother, pro-life leader, chairman of Eagle Forum

FEMINISM

Donna Steichen

> **Feminism is an ideological movement that sees women in families as akin to exploited workers in industrial factories: as a "domestic proletariat" that must engage in class struggle within the family rather than the workplace.**

You might be surprised to find an essay on Feminism included in this book. Like most Americans, you may assume that the feminist movement simply asserts that women are full members of the human race, equal to men in dignity and intellect, and equally deserving of opportunities to develop their gifts. In fact, Feminism is harder to pin down than many of the errors addressed by my fellow authors, because its advocates typically avoid defining the term. In consequence, "Feminism" takes on whatever color a listener gives it. So persistent is this ambiguity that, even now, few have more than a vague notion of its real nature.

Some highly reputable Catholics call themselves "pro-life feminists" and maintain that Feminism, if it could be purged of its attachment to abortion on demand, would be fundamentally good and compatible with the Faith.

Test Yourself: Are You a Feminist?

Few young women today aspire to emulate the ferocious, bra-burning militants of the 1960s. As mounting numbers of college students tell pollsters they question the morality of most abortions, old feminist slogans like "Abortion on Demand, Without Apology" make sane people wince. Nevertheless, most of us in the West have, often unwittingly, absorbed feminist premises that involve a wholesale re-evaluation of human nature and family life, and are in many respects incompatible with Christianity.

At its core, Feminism teaches that:

- Men and women tend to behave differently because of social conditioning, not because there are innate biological and psychological differences between them.

- The chief reason women have been less often represented in the first ranks of public achievement in scholarship, the arts, politics, and war, is that in every human society of which we have evidence, throughout all of recorded history, they were repressed by a patriarchal power structure maintained through force and indoctrination.

- Because large numbers of children in a family constitute both a barrier to the advancement of women and a threat to our ecology, small families should be the cultural norm.

- It is unjust that the consequences of sexual behavior are biologically unequal for men and women. As much as possible, those consequences must be equalized through medical technology and reformed cultural attitudes.

- To find meaning in their lives, women should look first to their careers, rather than to their role as lifegivers, culture bearers, nurturers, and educators of the next generation of human beings.

- Women who regard themselves as mothers first are wasting their education and smothering their talents by staying home to raise their children.

Thirty years of close study of Feminism in action, as well as reading hundreds of books written by its advocates, and attending scores of conferences held by feminists who called themselves Catholics (or at least "religious"), inform these conclusions. Reflect on them, and ask yourself honestly: does some part of you accept one or more of them? If so, then you have, to that degree, been infected with the feminist virus.

Our purpose here is not only to define Feminism but also to determine whether being a feminist is compatible with being a Christian. In any such assessment, an ideology must be judged by its "body count." We need not argue political theory with proponents of National Socialism; we can simply point to the Holocaust. Apologists for Soviet Communism must take into account the millions who perished in the gulag. Feminists, too, must evaluate an overwhelmingly ugly fact: since 1970, more than fifty million unborn American babies have died by their mother's choice at the hands of abortionists. That is Feminism's body count.

Feminism's Marxist Roots

A brief historical review helps to explain how Feminism was transformed from an eccentric opinion held by a few highly educated and discontented women to an ideology that revolutionized society's views about how to found families and how to live in them.

Make no mistake: Feminism has had that kind of power. And it has sought it. The leading "mainstream" feminist group in America, the National Organization for Women (NOW) said in its 1966 statement of goals that it would settle for nothing less than

> a sex role revolution for men and women which will restructure all our institutions: childrearing, education, marriage and the family, medicine, work, politics, the economy, religion, psychological theory, human sexuality, morality, and the very evolution of the race.[1]

Where did feminists get the idea that family life needed a "revolution"? From those specialists in revolution, the Marxists (see essay 13). In his 1884 treatise *The Origin of the Family, Private Property and the State,* Karl Marx's best friend and co-author, Frederich Engels, asserted that the "bourgeois" family with its division of labor—men working, women raising children—was one of the greatest obstacles to the achievement of a socialist society. Engels argued that this barrier should be dismantled by encouraging women to see themselves as an oppressed class, like exploited factory workers, who must engage in Marxist "class warfare" against their fathers and husbands. Of course, "class warfare" in the workplace has been condemned by numerous popes, including Leo XIII and Pius XI.[2] Applying that socialist principle to the intimate relations of the family is even more destructive: women who accept such a principle cease to see the family as a unit joined by common goals, and instead feel morally justified in seeking their own selfish interests—at the expense not just of their husbands but of their children. If a woman's own children can be her enemies, it is no wonder that feminists came to endorse first contraception and then abortion as central requirements for the progress of women in society.

From Class Struggle to Contraception

It is true, as "pro-life feminists" like to say, that early feminists like Susan B. Anthony and Elizabeth Cady Stanton accepted the belief, common in their era, that abortion is a barbaric crime committed by selfish men against women victims. Most nineteenth-century suffragists thought that women voters, with their presumably nobler morality, would heal a world wounded by male selfishness. But their fundamental premise—that women were an oppressed social class, a "domestic proletariat"—eventually eroded the wholesome social principles they had inherited from a deeply Christian society. Today, there is not a single major feminist organization that does not support government-funded contraception and abortion on demand. Opposing either of those demands gets women drummed out of such organizations, just as pro-life female candidates for office find themselves opposed by such high-powered feminist fundraising groups as Emily's List—whose litmus test is support for *Roe v. Wade*.

Even in its Victorian stages, Feminism's implicit assumption, that wives and husbands are opponents locked in a power struggle, was corrosive of society. The words of suffragist leaders reveal that, like Engels and Marx, they wanted to do away with traditional family roles. The suffragists did not call on society to value woman's distinctive and irreplaceable contributions as mothers and teachers of young people—who sometimes, out of necessity, had to work outside the home. Instead, they called on women to reject their natural vocation in order to live like men. In 1868, suffragist leader Elizabeth Cady Stanton, herself a married mother of seven, advocated birth control and equated traditional marriage with prostitution. She went on to say:

> Our idea is that every woman of sound mind and body, with brains and two hands, is more noble, virtuous, and happy in supporting herself. So long as a woman is dependent on a man, her relation to him will be a false one, either in marriage or out of it; she will despise herself and hate him whose desires she gratifies for the necessities of life; the children of such unions must needs be unloved and deserted.[3]

A libertarian might suppose Feminism to be merely a strategy to give women more options, enabling those not called to motherhood to achieve other highly-valued positions in society. Alas, no. For women who don't embrace their agenda, feminists tend to advocate coercion instead of liberty. Simone de Beauvoir, author of the pioneering feminist work *The Second Sex*, admitted as much in 1975:

> [A]s long as the family and the myth of the family and the myth of maternity and the maternal instinct are not destroyed, women will still be oppressed ... No woman should be authorized to stay at home and raise her children. Society should be totally different. Women should not have that choice, precisely because if there is such a choice, too many women will make that one. It is a way of forcing women in a certain direction.[4]

The Catholic Alternative

In contrast to the bleak vision of family life held by feminists, the Church has always taught that the family, not the individual, is the basic unit of society. Children are gifts from God, to be cherished in love and educated for life in Christ, and a just society must ensure that a mother has adequate means to stay home with her children, doing that irreplaceable work. Because of this, as Leo XIII and Pius XI wrote with papal authority,[5] a working man has a right in justice to a living wage—that is, a salary that can support his family in decent comfort. Indeed, as Allan Carlson documents in *The Family Way,*[6] by the end of the Second World War, most American employers—influenced by politically-active Catholics close to Franklin Roosevelt— were paying "family wages"—that is, offering higher wages to married men with children than to single or childless employees. The practice prevailed widely until 1964, when it was outlawed as "sex discrimination" by the Civil Rights Act. Ironically, that otherwise valuable legislation stripped from every mother the basic right to be supported as she cares for her baby—and replaced it with the feminist objective of uniform pay for anonymous workers in factories or offices.

From Contraception to Abortion

In the context of the times, it is not surprising that birth control crusader Margaret Sanger found her most eager recruits among the feminists of the 1920s. They sought, as she did, to reduce the "plague" of large families among the "less fit" immigrant ethnic groups who were filling up America's cities. Feminists who shared Sanger's eugenic concern for creating a "higher" human race through selective breeding influenced the passage of laws in thirteen American states requiring sterilization for those who fell below a certain norm on IQ tests. Feminists who did not join in Sanger's eugenic crusade were nevertheless led by concern for female autonomy to champion the use of contraceptive devices in marriage.[7] Practices once confined to prostitutes were now hailed as the key to happy marriage, by organizations with innocuous sounding names like "Women's Health Project," "Family Planning Associates" and, most well-known, "Planned Parenthood."

Inspired in part by feminist arguments, the Church of England in 1930 became the first Christian denomination in history to endorse the use of artificial birth control. Even well-meaning Christians, misled by such propaganda, joined notorious public figures and philanthropic foundations as Planned Parenthood benefactors. Donors' names range from advice columnist Abigail Van Buren to Johnny Carson, Senator Barry Goldwater, Bill and Melinda Gates, Barbra Streisand, Ted Turner, and Jane Fonda. Eventually, most other churches followed the Anglican example, leaving a single holdout—the Catholic Church.

Yet, by the late 1950s and early 1960s, many Catholics—consciously or not—had also accepted the feminist premise that women must be freed from the "burden" of frequent child-bearing to take their place alongside men as breadwinners. During the late 1960s, in the wake of changes introduced in the name of the Second Vatican Council (some authorized, many improvised), it was widely expected that Pope Paul VI would grant permission for Catholics to use artificial birth control. Promoters urged the Church to approve "the Pill," a recently invented form of hormonal contraception. The argument wouldn't have gained traction if it had been generally known then that the Pill doesn't always prevent conception, but instead can cause an early abortion.

In 1968, to general consternation, Pope Paul VI issued the historic encyclical *Humanae Vitae,* reaffirming the Church's two-thousand year teaching that marital relations are naturally ordered toward reproduction and that we may not employ artificial means to frustrate either the *procreative* or the *unitive* purposes of the sexual act. In the document, the pope issued grave warnings about the consequences likely to follow pervasive acceptance of contraception. His prophecies were casually dismissed—but almost all of them have come to pass.

Badly advised by dissenting priests, theologians, and even bishops, most American Catholics rejected the Church's teaching, and secular society proceeded along the path Paul VI had warned against. Among a majority of Catholics, expectations about marriage have been formed by secular culture and feminist ideology, not by the Church's teaching on lifelong sacramental union. Separating sexual pleasure from procreation led to the degradation of women and the cheapening of sex. Premarital sex became routine; unmarried cohabitation, unwed pregnancy, and single parenthood were soon accepted in every social class. In large sections of our population, fatherless families are now the norm.[8] Sexually-transmitted diseases and consequent infertility are pandemic. More than at any time since late pagan Rome, society nonchalantly tolerates sexual exploitation, abortion, and pornography. Children are sexualized at ever younger ages, as provocative clothing is marketed toward girls still below the age of puberty, and "comprehensive sex education" instructs elementary school students in perversions. Divorce and remarriage have lost any social stigma, even among Catholics: the Vatican has had to intervene to stem a deluge of casually granted annulments.

Single mothers with children make up the majority of the newly poor. Three generations of latch-key children have grown up neglected, emotionally stunted victims of fatherlessness and inadequate mothering, in a culture warped into moral confusion by perverse sex education, doctrinally empty religious instruction, coarsely sexualized television, and raw pornography online. For the first time in our history, married women are more likely to be employed than married men, and according to the 2007 U.S. Census Bureau Report "Families and Living Arrangements,"[9] only one woman in four with children under fifteen stays home to care for them.

Was It Worth the Price?

Few families have benefited even financially from the loss of the full-time mother. The demise of the "family wage" means that it now takes two full-time workers to provide a living standard comparable to that once earned by a male breadwinner. So most women remain trapped in the labor force out of economic need, trying to raise their children in their spare time. On that point, feminists like Simone de Beauvoir got what they wanted.

Explaining why he became a Catholic, G.K. Chesterton, wittiest of English converts, once wrote that the Faith "… is the only thing that frees a man from the degrading slavery of being a child of his age."[10] What the Faith offers in place of transient fads is the perennial truth about the human condition: why God made us, what kind of lives He wants us to live, what choices will lead us to the eternal happiness He intends for us. The Church knows that men and women are not interchangeable units. God created them in two sexes so they can unite in voluntary, permanent, loving, sacramental marriage covenants, and there raise up souls to God. It is hardly necessary to point out the mother's irreplaceable role in that enterprise.

Consistently, the popes have called the relationship between husband and wife one of equality in dignity and complementarity in function. Pope John Paul II was ridiculed when he cautioned men not to treat their wives as objects of lust, though what he advocated was the very mutuality feminists claim they seek.[11]

The sole advantage of living in a lawless time is that you can refuse to be a child of your age. Almost everyone in this workers' society is too preoccupied with his own place on the treadmill to pay much attention to your eccentricities. What devastated our culture was the flight of mothers from their homes. Society is drowning in the consequences, but nothing prevents you and your family from living your lives differently. Our culture will never be restored until women again take up rearing their children as their chief and indispensable task—and men make the sacrifices needed to support them in that decision. While aggressive forces continue to push the nation toward family disintegration, a healthy resistance movement is awake and growing. It is made up of uncompromising religious believers, pro-lifers, and homeschoolers, both organized and autonomous, along with back-to-the-land agrarians and Tea Party independents. One Virginia women's organization summed things up in a bumper sticker reading "Be Countercultural: Raise Your Own Kids."

An appetite for achievement is built into human nature. If women choose to model their lives on the Valiant Woman of Proverbs (31:10-31) by raising and educating their children in a genuinely Christian environment, they will have to find ways to present them with a culture no longer found in society's mainstream. This will be their most demanding, most absorbing, most gratifying task, requiring all their gifts, but eminently worth doing. Human imperfection always makes the future uncertain, but choosing freedom offers you and your family the best hope of finding joy in a deeply Catholic life.

Donna Steichen's first book, Ungodly Rage: The Hidden Face of Catholic Feminism, *stirred up a storm among feminists when it was published in 1991. Her most recent book is* Chosen: How Christ Sent Twenty-Three Surprised Converts to Replant His Vineyard.

Recommended Reading

√ *Domestic Tranquility: A Brief Against Feminism,* by F. Carolyn Graglia (Dallas: Spence Publishing, 1998).

√ *Men and Marriage,* by George Gilder (Gretna, LA: Pelican Publishing, 1992).

√ *The Way Home: Beyond Feminism, Back to Reality,* by Mary Pride (Wheaton, IL: Crossway Books, 1985).

√ *Feminist Fantasies: A True Female Success Story,* by Phyllis Schlafly (Dallas: Spence Publishing, 2003).

√ *A Return to Modesty: Discovering the Lost Virtue,* by Wendy Shalit (Austin, TX: Touchstone, 2000).

Notes

[1] As cited in *The New Freedom: Individualism and Collectivism in the Social Lives of Americans* by William A. Donohue (New Brunswick, NJ: Transaction Publishers, 1990), 59.

[2] See Leo XIII, *Rerum Novarum*, no. 19; Pius XI, *Divini Redemptoris*, no. 9.

[3] Elizabeth Cady Stanton, in *The Revolution*, viii, March 1868. For Stanton's support for contraception, see Jean H. Baker, *Sisters: The Lives of America's Suffragists* (New York: Hill and Wang, 2005), 106-109.

[4] "Sex, Society, and the Female Dilemma," *Saturday Review,* June 14, 1975.

[5] See Leo XIII, *Rerum Novarum*, no. 65; Pius XI, *Quadrigesimo Anno*, no. 71.

[6] Wilmington, DE: Intercollegiate Studies Institute Books, 2003.

[7] For a full history, see *Blessed Are the Barren: The Social Policy of Planned Parenthood*, by Robert G. Marshall and Charles A. Donovan (San Francisco: Ignatius Press, 1991).

[8] There are countless studies supporting these grim assertions. For a brief overview, see "The Decline of Marriage," by James Q. Wilson (*www.manhattan-institute.org/html/_sduniontrib-the_decline.htm*). For much more information, visit *www.marriagedebate.com*.

[9] See *www.census.gov/population/www/socdemo/hh-fam.html*

[10] G.K. Chesterton, *The Catholic Church and Conversion* (San Francisco: Ignatius Press, 2006), originally published in 1926.

[11] *Mulieris Dignitatem*, no. 10

senior Dreamworlds

"Insofar as he makes use of his healthy senses, man himself is the best and most exact scientific instrument possible. The greatest misfortune of modern physics is that its experiments have been set apart from man, as it were; physics refuses to recognize nature in anything not shown by artificial instruments, and even uses this as a measure of its accomplishments."
– Goethe, poet, scientist, author, *Faust*

SCIENTISM

John W. Keck

> **Scientism is simply an exaggerated belief in science. Scientism claims that the methods of the modern natural sciences provide our only access to the world and give the only kind of "truth."**

A civilization's conception of nature determines how it lives. Ours is no different. Just as the modern West depends for its prosperity on technology, modern ideologies draw their premises from the misunderstanding of science that is Scientism. It was the twentieth century that brought the full flowering of Scientism in the form of "scientific" racism and eugenics, "scientific Communism," and other totalitarian movements. It is true that the Second World War, the Holocaust, and the invention of nuclear weapons awakened many to the dangers entailed in abusing science. But the underlying errors that made possible all those modern horrors remain fixed in most of our minds. Even now, Scientism eats away at our civilization's foundations and destabilizes the institutions that protect and nourish human life.

Every falsehood with any traction is a perversion of a truth, and Scientism is no different. The truth in this case is the tremendous power for prediction and control that modern science has brought to mankind. It is undeniable that without science, we would still be at the mercy of the elements. But science, like everything else in the world, does have its limits. Those who ignore these limits and unduly inflate the value of science are the devotees of Scientism. We need to understand the real limits of science to avoid embracing their world view, which essentially amounts to a new and false religion.

What Is Science? The Limits of Science

The word "science" comes from the Latin word for knowledge, *scientia*, and originally applied to any organized field of knowledge. Theology and philosophy especially were known as sciences, and for most of the history of Western civilization, "science" was roughly synonymous with "philosophy."

All that sounds odd to us now. Any elementary school child who watches Hollywood movies *knows* that these disciplines lack two key characteristics of science: madly scribbled chalk-board equations and white lab coats. By the late nineteenth century, "science" became restricted to the natural sciences such as astronomy, physics, chemistry, and biology—and also to "social sciences" such as politics and psychology, but only insofar as they relied on methods characteristic of the natural sciences. There are many ways of knowing, but the modern "scientific way" is characteristically *mathematical* and *experimental*. This nicely clarifies matters—and limits, we should note, what kind of things *can ever be known* "scientifically." If we assert (as Scientism does) that no other mode of knowledge is valid, then we are dismissing vast areas of life as permanently unknowable.

Mathematics can only deal with things that can be counted or measured. The great power of mathematics is that its results are completely general and apply to all sorts of things. Addition works with bananas just as well as it works for bricks. But this power is also precisely its limitation: in being completely general, mathematics is not specific to any particular thing. In other words, mathematics does not deal with what things *are*—it completely abstracts from such questions and deals only with their quantity. As Bertrand Russell (1872–1970) once wrote of modern mathematics, "Thus mathematics may be defined as the subject in which we never know what we are talking about, nor whether what we are saying is true."[1]

In modern science, we answer that question by using the experimental method. Notice what a peculiar way of knowing experiment is. Unlike simple observation, experiments are controlled situations. Immanuel Kant (1724–1804) well described the difference between the experimental method and the classical mode of passively observing nature:

> Thus reason must indeed approach nature in order to be instructed by it; yet it must do so not in the capacity of a pupil who lets the teacher tell him whatever the teacher wants, but in the capacity of an appointed judge who compels the witnesses to answer the questions that he puts to them.[2]

Experiment interrogates nature to make her give up her secrets. So it should be no surprise that sometimes experiment yields a different answer than simple observation. Dissecting a frog tells you different things than watching a live frog behaving spontaneously in its natural habitat. In reality, simple observation is just as important as the artifice of experiment: they are complementary ways of exploring the world. Nature passively observed may not disclose as many secrets, but those she does will be more genuine, less contrived. That is why naturalists travel to wild habitats to observe animals living in nature.

Science has tremendous power for the "prediction and control" of nature. Experiment is the perfect tool of this approach. In the experimental method, investigators formulate a *hypothesis* whose consequences they test against experimental results. If the results match the predictions of the hypothesis, then the hypothesis wins an additional degree of confirmation. The process of confirming hypotheses isn't infallible. Ptolemy's earth-centered system predicted the positions of the planets far more accurately than Copernicus' heliocentric system—yet Copernicus' system was closer to reality. For hundreds of years, Newton's cosmic framework was considered the last word on the operations of the physical world, as confirmed by every experimental test. Then, in the twentieth century, it became clear that Newton's system, while insightful, was not strictly speaking *true*: it merely made correct predictions in a wide range of situations. Quantum mechanics and Einsteinian relativity superseded Newtonian mechanics; yet there is no guarantee that they too will not be superseded by better theories (and indeed at least one must be, since they are mutually incompatible).

A key point to notice is that models, strictly speaking, apply to the *controlled circumstances* of experiments. Thus, experimentation doesn't so much discover truths about the natural world, as it tests how to reliably *make particular things happen under human-controlled conditions*. The most elaborate of these human contrivances are called machines. The experimental method subtly leads its practitioners to approach nature as they would a machine.

The basic difference between traditional and modern science is one of attitude: whereas the ancients and medievals sought *truth*, moderns primarily seek *control*. Experiment can indicate how nature acts in herself, but primarily it tells us how nature acts *under human control*. How did science come to equate control with truth?

The Origins of Scientism

Scientism was born with science, as its dark twin—or perhaps more aptly, as its shadow. A coarse sketch of the historical background will make the situation clearer. The Middle Ages saw the rediscovery of the thought of the ancients. Aristotle, in particular, was held in high regard as a result of the monumental work of St. Thomas Aquinas (1225–1274). In the later Middle Ages, philosophy and other sciences decayed, as thinkers rested on the success of their earlier years, rehashing old texts and principles instead of looking to the sensible world. Aristotle's (and hence Aquinas') theory of knowledge, "nothing in the intellect not first in the senses," was unfortunately obscured by thinkers such as William of Occam (c.1288–c.1348). Blessed Duns Scotus (c.1265–1308) unwittingly opened a new front in the conflict between faith and reason by putting God on the same level of existence as creatures.[3] The Renaissance saw a further recovery of classical texts including Plato and the pre-Socratics, which to many made the achievements of the medievals appear provincial and unenlightened. The increasing wealth of Europe also widened the separation between man and non-human nature. The time was ripe for revolt.

This was the intellectual pre-history of the Scientific Revolution. Niccolò Machiavelli (1469–1527) and Peter Ramus (1515–1572) were early activists for casting off the old authorities. But three men—Francis Bacon (1561–1626), Galileo Galilei (1564–1642), and Rene Descartes (1596–1650)—are known as the master architects of the Scientific Revolution.

Science is a human institution, so it should be no surprise to realize that the scientific project is as much political as it is intellectual. Francis Bacon was above all a politician, contributing not as much to scientific methods as to science's self-conception. He sought to throw off traditional or *received* wisdom[4] such as Greek philosophy—which he dismissed as having "the characteristic property of boys: it can talk, but it cannot generate; for it is fruitful of controversies but barren of works."[5] What sort of "works" does Bacon mean? Later, he says that the "true ends of knowledge" are "the benefit and use of life" and that his intention is to "lay the foundation ... of human utility and power."[6] Elsewhere, Bacon promises the reader that he is "come in very truth leading to you Nature with all her children to bind her to your service and make her your slave."[7]

Descartes likewise rejected scholastic philosophy, arguing that Aristotle's principles could be dismissed because "no progress has been attained by their means in all the centuries in which they have been followed."[8] In other words, it is only a philosophy's *consequences* that justify it. And the central consequence of concern is *power*. Descartes wrote that the overriding purpose of all science is to "render ourselves the masters and possessors of nature."[9]

The men we might call the "scientific revolutionaries" thus denigrated knowledge sought for its own sake. Knowledge that "merely" gave man a better idea of his place in the universe was useless and hence worthless. Bacon's assertion that "knowledge is power" has become cliché. For Scientism, power is the ultimate purpose.

Can Science Be Its Own Foundation?

The funny thing about Scientism as preached by its progenitors Descartes and Bacon is that it is, on its own terms, *unscientific*. Look at the claim they make—that the only things we can know are those "proven" by mathematics or experiments. This claim itself cannot be tested by either one—so, on "scientific" grounds, it is unproveable, an article of *faith*. We can also see the falsehood of Scientism by looking at the nature of science. The practice of modern science relies on many presumptions, such as the *existence of a world outside our minds*, the *regularity of universal laws*, and the *ability of the human mind to discover those laws*. Since science *rests* on these assumptions, it cannot prove them without assuming what it sets out to prove—in other words, arguing in a circle.

Even more broadly, science depends on general philosophical considerations. These philosophical conclusions are reasoned from common experiences shared by every adult. Science cannot reject these conclusions without undermining itself. That means that these things are *more certain* than science. In a lecture[10] he gave at the Massachusetts Institute of Technology, philosopher Michael Augros asked his audience to consider two statements:

Statement (1)   Some things move.

Statement (2)   Light moves at 2.99792458×10^8 m/s.

He then asked, 'Which statement is more specific? Which is more certain?' The first statement is more vague and general, but for that reason it is also more certain. Notice the logical relationship between the statements: it cannot be true that light has a particular speed unless it moves, which means "some things move." So the first statement has to be more certain. What is more, all adults have an experience of motion, whereas very few of us have measured the speed of light (or even seen the specialized equipment needed for doing so). So there is an element of faith (that is, reliance on credible authorities) in (2) that is not present in (1). There are many more dependable observations like (1), and they form the unique experiential base of natural philosophy. The critical point here is that we have access to reality *outside* of modern scientific methods—science itself requires it.

Another common experience is of natural wholes, such as rhododendra and rhinoceri, but also of ourselves. One of the many errors that Scientism begets is *mechanism*, which treats natural wholes like mere machines, that is juxtapositions of unrelated parts, assembled from without by an external intelligence. Mechanism rejects the existence of things with inherent activities and tendencies. Isaac Newton (1643–1727) is seen as the great proponent of the mechanical conception of the universe ("a great clockwork"), but Descartes, who taught that matter's only property was occupying space, was more thoroughly mechanistic. He actually believed and taught that animals were merely machines—an assertion that made later scientists more willing to engage in vivisection experiments we would consider cruel. How could a machine be said to suffer? Many modern biochemists have unthinkingly extended this assumption to human beings, which is one reason why so few researchers feel ethical qualms about experimenting on human embryos.[11]

The Ultimate Frame

A given person can believe in two things whose compatibility is, to put it mildly, not immediately obvious. For example, modern "educated" people believe that man is a mere creature in an environment, the product of blind forces in an unintelligent universe. At the same time, they also accept the idea of human rights. But the notion that we have rights arose from a vision of man that is very different—one that implies we are somehow special in the universe. This assertion comes from the old belief that human beings were created by God in His image. Both pictures of man cannot be true. So which do we accept?

The control aspect of science strengthens the inclination to reduce other men to the status of animals. The invisible partner to any scientific notion is the human self, a disembodied observer standing beyond anything observable. If "science" is the ultimate frame of reality, then the human self stands beyond all that is, in a God-like position.[12] Religious belief in this scientific age hinges on this question: Is the universe described by modern science part of a much larger reality, a mysterious Beyond that we will never actually master, or is "belief" in a Beyond just another incidental feature of the universe described by modern science, a by-product of physical processes but referring to nothing real? What is *your* ultimate frame? You or Something Greater?

Even if our beliefs are ambiguous, our lives answer the question. Is the premise underlying our actions the belief that *we* are the sole source of reality and everything else exists purely for our use, or that we are part of a much larger reality, a reality that makes demands on us? Do we treat everything else in the universe, especially other people, as existing purely for our pleasure, or do we guide our lives in light of a much larger reality? Our lives are the ultimate experiment, and its results will leave no doubt.

John W. Keck teaches at the Concourse Program at the Massachusetts Institute of Technology (MIT). He received his doctorate in physics from Columbia University and is a fellow of the Institute for the Study of Nature (<u>www.isnature.org</u>).

Recommended Reading

√ *A Student's Guide to Philosophy*, by Ralph M. McInerny (Wilmington, DE: Intercollegiate Studies Institute Books, 1999).

√ *The Last Superstition*, by Edward Feser (South Bend, IN: St. Augustine's Press, 2007).

√ *The Phenomenon of Life: Toward a Philosophical Biology*, by Hans Jonas (Evanston, IL: Northwestern University Press, 1966).

√ *Matter and Becoming*, by Richard J. Connell (Chicago: The Priory Press, 1966).

√ *Physics*, by Aristotle (Princeton, NJ: Princeton University Press, 1984).

Notes

[1] "Recent Work on the Principles of Mathematics," *International Monthly* 4 (1901).

[2] Immanuel Kant, *Critique of Pure Reason*, trans. Werner S. Pluhar (Mineola, NY: Dover, 1996), 19.

[3] Brad S. Gregory, "Science Versus Religion?: The Insights and Oversights of the 'New Atheists'," *Logos* 12:4 (Fall 2009), 17–55.

[4] Cf. Yuval Levin, "Science and the Left," *The New Atlantis* (Winter 2008).

[5] Francis Bacon, "The Great Instauration," 8, available online at *www. constitution.org/bacon/instauration.htm* .

[6] Ibid., 16

[7] "The Masculine Birth of Time" in Benjamin Farrington, *The Philosophy of Francis Bacon* (Chicago: University of Chicago Press, 1964), 62.

[8] Rene Descartes, *Principles of Philosophy*, 19

[9] Rene Descartes, "Discourse on the Method," part VI, 62, trans. Elizabeth S. Haldane and G.R.T. Ross, ed. Enrique Chavez-Arvizo, *Descartes: Key Philosophical Writings* (Ware, UK: Wordsworth Editions, 1997), 111.

[10] Michael Augros, "A 'Bigger' Physics" (lecture January 28, 2009 at Massachusetts Institute of Technology).

[11] Cf. Richard Stith, "Arresting Development: Human Beings Don't Roll Off an Assembly Line," *Touchstone* 21:1 (Jan-Feb 2008), 32-35.

[12] Walker Percy, *Lost in the Cosmos: The Last Self-Help Book* (New York: Picador, 2000).

"America is a nation with the soul of a church."
– G. K.Chesterton, novelist, Catholic convert and apologist

AMERICANISM

Mark Shea

> Americanism is the tendency, condemned by Pope Leo
> XIII, to put conformity with American culture and
> politics before the teachings of the universal Church.

Chances are that your professors feel differently about patriotism than you do. Most of them came of age in the era of Vietnam and Watergate, when "enlightened" people agreed that love of country, military service, pledges of allegiance and flags were at best passé, and at worst might be symptoms of "fascism." But the Baby Boom generation was fighting against human nature itself, which drives us to love our native land. Many Americans woke up to this reality in the wake of 9/11, when the agonies of that day showed again how fragile is the security we enjoy in a dangerous world and how much we owe our country and the brave men and women who have committed their lives to defending it and us. Those of you who have grown up in the shadow of 9/11 think differently about patriotism than your teachers. And you are right.

History is on your side. Athenians loved Athens, Spartans loved Sparta, and Romans loved Rome. As the nation-state came into being, patriotism—the primal love of home—fueled the process as the English came to love England, the French France, the Spaniards Spain—and Americans to love America. As St. Thomas Aquinas taught, such gratitude is a fitting response to one's country: for it, like your parents, gives you all sorts of things—an education, a culture, a language, a stable civil order, an economy from which to benefit, and an infinitude of other gifts—that you could not possibly have produced for yourself from scratch.

That is why patriotism is at once natural and obligatory on pain of sin, like loving your own mother and father—because it is loving your own mother and father, and your grandmother and grandfather, too. True patriotism is unconditional love. You do not love your parents because they are better than other people's parents. You love them because they are yours: the people God has given you to love. God loves us because he is Love, not because we have done something to earn it. Our task as Christians is to imitate this in all our loves, including the love of country.

Unconditional love is a funny thing, and easy to misinterpret. Sometimes family members will lie for each other under oath, or cover up when a loved one does something wrong. Clearly, that isn't what God does for us—or else everybody, from Judas to Hitler, at death would go straight to heaven. So it must be a distortion. Likewise, it is a distortion when patriotic people assert, "My country, right or wrong."

Love vs. Pride

Unconditional love for one's country does not mean approving everything its government does, but loving your country in obedience to God. When your government disobeys God, love of country means calling it to repent, not approving its sin. The prophets did this— and paid with their lives. But the prophets were great patriots. So was Jesus when He denounced Jerusalem for killing the prophets, stoning those sent to her, and refusing to accept His message (Matthew 23). He was deeply patriotic for Israel, because He was first a patriot of the kingdom of heaven. In short, He was a patriot, but not a nationalist.

What's the difference? Here lies the gulf between love and pride, the difference between worshipping God and an idol. Idolatry occurs the instant we put a creature before the Creator, and make of it a false god. And that is what nationalism does. We must not treat our beloved flag like a Golden Calf.

What pride is to a person, nationalism is to a people. Sooner or later, every people seems to hit the point where, under the influence of pride, they want to feel as though they occupy a more special and privileged place in the divine plan than all other nations. In this, they imitate the only ethnic group that ever really had a valid claim to be Chosen: the children of Israel. But the paradox of biblical election is this: the Chosen are always chosen for the sake of the Unchosen. This is what God is getting at when he tells Abraham "through you all the nations of the earth will be blessed" (Genesis 12:3). And that imposes a terrible burden on any who would aspire to such a terrible blessing. For if you are chosen for the sake of the unchosen, the day must inevitably come where it is required that you give up your life that another may live, since all (including the Jews) are chosen in Christ and for His plans and purposes, not theirs (Ephesians 1:4).

So to be chosen is to be called to walk in the way of Christ, which is the way of death and resurrection, not political triumphalism. Sooner or later, you must make a choice: lay down your life—or not. When that choice is required, you can instead choose the mystery of evil and say, with Caiaphas, "It is better that one man die than that a whole nation should perish" (John 11:50). Like John and James, nations can and often have sought to have a place at the right and left hand of Christ. To them, our Lord has always replied, "You do not know what you are asking" (Mark 10:35-45).

Every nation wants to be the Chosen People, at some point in their history. Again and again, we see nations, in their prime, desiring to be a royal priesthood, a chosen nation, and a people set apart. Each of the great nations of Europe seem to have gone through this phase. We see it reflected in the myth of the Grail in England and the notion that Jesus took time out of His busy schedule to pay some boyhood visits to Britain:

> *And did those feet in ancient time,*
> *Walk upon England's mountains green:*
> *And was the holy Lamb of God,*
> *On England's pleasant pastures seen!*
> ("Jerusalem," William Blake)

England even started its own church (the Anglican) for its king to rule over as pope.

Likewise, when France was in peak form, she claimed the title "Eldest Daughter of the Church" (that's before she went to Paris, took an atheist lover, and started reading Voltaire and Sartre). French bishops resisted papal authority, and earned the title of "Gallicans." Russia too, had its spasm of Christo-nationalism in the nineteenth century when it claimed the title of "Christ of the Nations." In the 1930s, Germany embraced an extremely debased notion of being a Chosen People with catastrophic results, proving once again that nothing is more dangerous than a single biblical idea cut off from the rest of revelation. Soviet Russia likewise proclaimed itself the redemptive nation on behalf of the global working class—Karl Marx's new chosen race (see essay 13, "Marxism").

The American Temptation

Has America been immune? Sadly, no. From the Pilgrim's City on a Hill, to the Founders' *Novus Ordo Seclorum* ("A New Order of the Ages") to Lincoln's Second Inaugural to the theory of Manifest Destiny to George W. Bush's "New World Order," Bill Clinton's "New Covenant," to the current anointing of President Barack Obama as a sort of messianic king by his disciples, American politics is suffused with the constant tendency to confuse the Kingdom of Heaven and the American Way. Not for nothing did G.K. Chesterton remark that we are a nation with the "soul of a church." Nor was it an oversight that led Pope Leo XIII to condemn as a heresy something called "Americanism," which we will explore below.

Evangelical Christians, not having a visible Church to warn them away, are especially prone to make of America a New Israel, and in the '70s and '80s they churned out books stating specifically "what the Bible says" about America's "role" in God's plan. There is only one problem with doing this: The Bible doesn't say anything about America's role in God's plan. The only ethnic group that figures in God's plan is the Jewish people. And the only successor to the Jews we find in the Bible is the Church—which is, as Paul tells us, the Israel of God (see 1 Corinthians 10:6; Galatians 6:16).

The notion of America as a Chosen Nation is something that brings out the best—and the worst—in us. It inspired us to do great and noble things out of real self-sacrificial heroism—and it fills us with incredibly obnoxious hubris. It prompted us to storm the beaches of Normandy, save Berlin from the Commies, and found things like the Peace Corps. But, because our Puritan missionary spirit goes marching on even when our culture degrades into complete apostasy, we continue our sense of mission even when the mission becomes to export abortion and pornographic pop culture as far as humanly possible. It gets tough to cling to the myth of a redemptive America when your chief cultural exports are Lady Gaga and condoms.[1]

For Catholics, the situation is rife with confusion, too. American Catholics live in a culture which, for centuries, has succeeded in giving us an enviable standard of living compared to most of the world. Gratitude for that is only right. But along with that great gift has come a hefty price tag: the long, slow pressure to sign-on for what Pope Leo XIII called the heresy of "Americanism,"[2] that is, the worship of America as an idol.

Dr. John Rao's classic treatise sums up the tenets of our national temptation:

> Americanism is a term that appears to express nothing more than a devotion to America. In reality, however, it teaches principles and a way of life that pose, and always have posed, a threat to the Church of Rome. Indeed, the threat that it poses to Catholicism may be the most dangerous experienced by her in the past few centuries of revolution. Its harmful quality arises from its subtle and effective transformation of the United States into a new religion whose central dogma of "pluralism" cannot be investigated or questioned; a new religion whose creed is said to be purely "practical" and "pragmatic," but which actually aims at a messianic rebuilding of the entire globe; a new religion that brooks no opposition to its will.[3]

Americanism attacks the ultimate claims on our allegiance made by Christ through his holy Church. It insists that we sublimate the Catholic faith to the need to be an Ordinary American who accepts "pluralism." But this means not mere religious freedom (something the Church herself affirms in her *Decree on Religious Freedom*[4]) but indifferentism. True religious freedom means that while error has no rights, persons in error do have rights. So you are entitled to your opinion in good conscience, even when that opinion is mistaken or mixed with error. Efforts may be made to correct wrong ideas and inculcate right ones as long as they respect the dignity of the person.

In contrast, indifferentism means that each person is entitled to his own truth and that there is no truth to be wrong about. Instead of God as the highest good, being a good American becomes the highest good. This is the insidious compromise which Pope Leo XIII was already fighting in the nineteenth century when certain Catholics (including some bishops) were laboring to achieve total assimilation to Protestant America, even to the point of opposing the Catholic school system, while public schools were offering Protestant (and often deeply anti-Catholic) catechesis. It was a temptation that was embraced by millions of Catholics in the 1960s and after when they followed John F. Kennedy, who said in his campaign, in effect: "I am not a Catholic first and an American second. I am an American first, who happens also to be Catholic." Claims like "Jesus is the Way, the Truth and the Life and no one comes to the Father but by Him" become intolerable in such a civic culture—as did the Church's truth claims about herself and her mission. We are going to have trouble remaining indifferent to religious differences if we accept that the Church is telling the truth when she calls herself "the sacrament of salvation, the sign and the instrument of the communion of God and men."[5]

In Kennedy's blasé dismissal of his own faith, Catholics bought into the notion that their first duty was to America, not God, and this notion continues to infect Catholic Americans by the millions, whatever their political party affiliation. Catholic Leftists went along with Americanist notions that the "right" to an abortion trumped the commandment, "You shall not kill." Catholic Rightists bought into the notion that the City on the Hill could legitimately use nuclear weapons against civilians, and ignore the warnings of popes against launching needless wars. Again and again, American Catholics chose the perceived American way of life (small families, big houses, plain churches, fancy homes, hedonism, materialism, and militarism) over the Gospel. It's a powerful temptation—which is why most of us succumb to it. And it has such a pretty-sounding name: Americanism. Who wants to sound like he is being "un-American"?

Sins against Patriotism

Well, there are plenty of Leftists who are happy to embrace that stance, and who reject proper patriotism, throwing the baby out with the bathwater. For a minority of Catholics, the solution to Americanism has become anti-Americanism: an ungrateful contempt for America that despises her, her institutions, her people, her way of life, her liberties, her government and the very essence of who she is and what she stands for. Some Catholic extremists have hoped for her defeat in war, her economic ruin, even the destruction of her democratic institutions and the reinstitution of monarchy. This amounts to sinful ingratitude that is the mirror image of sinful nationalistic pride: both are the enemies of patriotism, which is the authentic love of country that stands subordinate to the love of God.

Of course, Catholic social teaching has always had a pretty good bead on primary and secondary goods. Love God and your neighbor are the two big commandments, in that order. Love of country is simply a corollary of the second greatest commandment. As long as the greatest commandment is Numero Uno, the second greatest can be followed with complete freedom. But the moment somebody tries to put the second commandment first, or cancel the second in favor of the first, is the moment a line has been crossed and true patriotism has been abandoned.

So the sacred and secular are clearly distinguished in the Catholic tradition. Render to Caesar what is Caesar's and to God what is God's. But when somebody tries to tell us to put the interests of Caesar before the command of God, or to get rid of Caesar and put God in his place, they are speaking with the voice of the devil or the theocratic fanatic.

Ultimately, our goals as a nation are not the same as those of the Church, who is the only fully fitting recipient of all that prophetic witness in Scripture about being a "chosen nation," etc. So Christians tempted by Americanism are often profoundly conflicted about America, because she goes on stubbornly being a purely temporal creature concocted by Enlightenment minds and subject to all the changes this world has to offer. They keep hoping she will fill the bill for the Church. But America is not the Church. She is only a nation with the soul of a church—a Calvinist church at that—and she has been exhaling that soul for some time now and breathing in lots of other spirits. She won't last forever. No merely human nation will. On the Last Day, the only two peoples we are guaranteed to still see standing will be the House of Israel and the Catholic Church, finally reconciled in their common Messiah.

But this is not a reason not to fight for America. Nor is it a reason to get rid of America and replace it with some sort of Catholic theocracy. Your mother won't last forever either, but that's hardly a reason to give up on her. Your mother is not God, but that doesn't mean you don't owe her honor. America is one of the greatest human inventions the world has ever seen: an *almost* sacred thing. But *only* almost. Great as she is, she remains a human invention, not the inspired creation of God, nor a light of revelation to the Gentiles nor the glory of His people Israel. That role has been filled for all time by Jesus Christ. So all the normal apostolic warnings about exalting human traditions to the level of the Tradition of God apply (see Mark 7:8; Colossians 2:8).

If we don't make that distinction between human and apostolic tradition, we wind up making one of two errors (or both):

1. We can get unjustly angry at America (or whatever other human thing we idolize) for being only human and not meeting our divine hopes. This is the blunder of Leftists enraged by America's failure to be the Kingdom of God.

2. We can accept the false hope that America is an adequate substitute for the Kingdom of God and accord America the allegiance due only to God and His Church.

In the end, Russell D. Moore sums it up well:

> There is a liberation theology of the Left, and there is also a liberation theology of the Right, and both are at heart mammon worship. The liberation theology of the Left often wants a Barrabas, to fight off the oppressors as though our ultimate problem were the reign of Rome and not the reign of death. The liberation theology of the Right wants a golden calf, to represent religion and to remind us of all the economic security we had in Egypt. Both want a Caesar or a Pharaoh, not a Messiah.[6]

But a Messiah is what we have, thanks be to God. Accept no substitutes.

Mark Shea is the author of numerous books, including the Mary, Mother of the Son *trilogy,* Making Senses Out of Scripture: Reading the Bible as the First Christians Did, *and* By What Authority? An Evangelical Discovers Catholic Tradition. *He blogs at* www.markshea.blogspot.com.

Recommended Reading

√ *Dignitatis Humanae* (*Decree on Religious Freedom*), from the Second
   Vatican Council; available online at *www.vatican.va/archive/
   hist_councils/ii_vatican_council/documents/vat-ii_decl_19651207_
   dignitatis-humanae_en.html*

√ *The Second Vatican Council and Religious Liberty,* by Michael Davies
   (Long Prairie, MN: The Neumann Press, 1992).

√ *The Roots of American Order,* by Russell Kirk (Chicago: Open Court
   Publishing, 1977).

√ *We Hold These Truths,* 2nd ed., by Fr. John Courtney Murray, SJ (New
   York: Sheed and Ward, 1986).

√ *Americanism and the Collapse of the Church in the United States,* by John
   C. Rao (Nashville: TAN, 1994).

Notes

1   See John Zmirak, "America the Abstraction," *The American
    Conservative,* January 13, 2003, available online at *www.amconmag.com/
    article/2003/jan/13/00008*

2   See *Testem Benevolentiae Nostrae,* available online at *www.ewtn.com/
    library/PAPALDOC/L13TESTE.HTM*

3   John C. Rao, *Americanism and the Collapse of the Church in the United
    States,* available online at *http://jcrao.freeshell.org/Americanism*

4   See Second Vatican Council, *Dignitatis Humanae,* available online at
    *www.vatican.va/archive/hist_councils/ii_vatican_council/documents/vat-
    ii_decl_19651207_dignitatis-humanae_en.html*

5   *Catechism of the Catholic Church,* no. 780

6   Russell D. Moore, "The Messiah Complex," *Touchstone Magazine,* July/
    August 2008, available online at *http://touchstonemag.com/archives/article.
    php?id=21-06-016-v*

"[A]lthough the socialists, stealing the very Gospel itself with a view to deceive more easily the unwary, have been accustomed to distort it so as to suit their own purposes, nevertheless so great is the difference between their depraved teachings and the most pure doctrine of Christ that none greater could exist: "For what participation hath justice with injustice or what fellowship hath light with darkness?" (2 Cor. 6:14)."

– Pope Leo XIII

Jeffrey Tucker

> Marxism is a philosophical system that asserts that the
> "real" explanation of most things that happen in society
> rests in the unequal relationships of money and/or power,
> which are inherently unjust and should be remedied by
> the use of force—either through a violent revolution that
> will impose equality, or through organizing society's
> "have-nots" to take political power and seize what is
> "rightly" theirs by means of taxation and regulation.

Every college student is sure to learn from his professors and
from campus activist groups the litany of sins that supposedly
condemn the Christian West: racism, sexism, elitism, environmental
degradation, and discrimination against a panoply of "victim" groups.
These accusations rest on a central premise: that all social relations are
based on conflict, with deep roots embedded in issues of class, race,
sex, religion, educational opportunity, and many other inequalities.
These conflicts can only be resolved by dramatic social, cultural, and
political upheaval that takes power away from "oppressor" groups (i.e.,
Christians, white males, business owners) and gives it to the "victims."

Or so they say. This view of society has its root in the thinking of
Karl Marx (1818–1883), the founder of "scientific socialism," the most
famous self-styled "communist." There were many radical socialists
before him, but what Marx added to their thought was the idea of

"class conflict," which remains his most influential legacy. For Marx, competition among men for status and success should not be seen as a natural part of human behavior—albeit one exaggerated and tainted by the effects of Original Sin, which tempts individuals to act unjustly toward their neighbors. (That is what the Church has always taught.)

In fact, for Marx, we shouldn't even be looking at individuals in the first place. The key to history is the struggle for power among different *groups*; each person in these groups (for instance, you and me) is of little significance. "Iron laws" of history drive whole classes of people—all the workers, all the businessmen, or all the women and all the men—into bitter conflicts that can only be resolved with one group overpowering and subjugating the other. This bleak view of human nature formed the revolutionary movements that would someday take power from Russia to North Korea. This theory of human relations justified the revolutionaries, in their own minds, in killing or imprisoning millions of their fellow men, starting wars, and persecuting anyone (for instance, Christians) who took a different view. While it may seem that Communism has been discredited by its large-scale collapse in 1989-90, in fact, Marx's theory of class conflict is still widely popular today—among intellectuals, professors, community organizers, and journalists. It even has many supporters among "progressive" members of the clergy.

A Zero-Sum Society

For these people—who may not admit or even realize that they are Marxists—all social relationships center on the *struggle for power*, which is won or lost depending on the *ownership of property*. You are either a member of the group that has power and property, or one of those trying to seize it. There is no room for division of labor, a natural hierarchy of talent, or cooperation among groups at different rungs of the social ladder. There are only winners and losers. Those at the bottom of the ladder must claw their way to the top, and pull down the people over them. The only way to end this cycle of conflict is to abolish private property and establish perfect equality; this task is so demanding that it can only be achieved by wielding absolute power. That is why Marx calls for a "dictatorship of the proletariat."

To make the revolution that will create this perfect society, oppressed people must become conscious of their plight, and of the necessity for abolishing private property. That is where activists come in, whose job is it to engage in a massive task of political consciousness raising. As Marx said, without these efforts, "it is not the consciousness of men that determines their existence, but their social existence that determines their consciousness." In other words, society's victims don't even realize that they are victims, until activists step in to wake them up. And one of the key ways to do that is to gain powerful positions in government, media, and on college campuses—then use those positions to spread the gospel of revolutionary change.

Thinking like Whitey

This means that any teacher you encounter who believes in Marxist theory isn't really trying to teach you to think for yourself about the subject matter of the class; he is trying to shape your thinking to promote his political agenda—for your own good, of course. At this point, you might ask, "What about objective Truth?" To which a good Marxist would answer that such a Truth does not exist. In fact, Marxists believe that members of different groups *don't even think the same way*—they don't share a common logical structure. Instead, the people in each group have grown up thinking according to the "logic" of their race, sex, or social class: "You only think that way because you're white."

The fact that people in different groups use different logical structures means that they cannot really cooperate; in fact, they are doomed to conflict. The powerful groups use their logic to exploit the weaker ones, and it is our duty to remedy this injustice, to use the power of the State to wipe out the privileges of the powerful. So pervasive is this conflict-based point of view that it will probably be taken for granted in most of your social science classes. In women's studies (see essay 10, "Feminism") the goal is the overthrow of the "patriarchy"; in black studies, the ruthless uncovering of "racism" in every corner of society; in sociology, the liberation of marginalized groups such as sexual outlaws and even criminals. Indeed, you're likely to find in your English classes that many teachers are mostly interested in looking for evidence that writers such as Shakespeare or Jane Austen were racist, sexist, or "ethnocentric."

If you were to disagree with a teacher for taking this approach, he will likely have a ready, Marxist answer: you lack the "proper consciousness." In fact, you are trapped in the logic of a privileged class, a captive of the "dead, white European males" who wrote most of the Great Books that colleges used to reverently teach (see essay 5, "Multiculturalism"). The idea that different groups have different logics (*polylogism*, from "multiple" + "logics") makes it difficult if not impossible to argue against "political correctness" on campus. If you suggest that women might rather choose motherhood over a career, and that this choice ought to be respected, you are accused of sexism. If you suggest that income disparities among the races in America aren't based entirely on discrimination, you are accused of racism. And so on. Rarely is an argument given to back up these claims. Rather, the person who offers a different point of view is merely dismissed as an apologist for the exploiters—and frequently punished. Students who reject Marxist arguments can end up with lower grades; professors who dissent can lose their jobs. It happens more often than you would think.

The High Price of Cheap Debating Tricks

This Marxist tactic, of asserting multiple logics, amounts to nothing more than an *ad hominem* attack—rejecting what someone says based not on its truth or falsehood, but on irrelevant facts concerning the person who says it. Yet Marxists have been using this ploy, and getting away with it, for more than a century. A classic example can be found in *Karl Marx and the Close of His System* by Austrian economist Eugen von Böhm-Bawerk in 1896.[1] Böhm-Bawerk offered a painstakingly detailed argument, stretching over 150 pages, that Marx was wrong about his most fundamental economic principle—the "labor theory of value." According to Marx, we value something based on how much work went into making it. So a car that takes 300 man-hours to manufacture is worth more than one that took only 100 hours. If a businessman running the plant makes a profit, he is essentially stealing it from the workers—whose labor added all the value people are paying for. Böhm-Bawerk pointed out how Marx's theory leaves out many factors from the equation—for instance, the skill of managers, the quality of the work, the money it took to buy first-rate tools and design a car that actually runs, and so on. These things, and not the simple number of hours it takes factory workers to assemble something, make all the difference between a jalopy and a Jaguar. We don't price cars based on how hard people worked to make them, any more than a teacher grades a paper based on how many hours each student spent writing it.

Böhm-Bawerk further writes that Marxism seems to have built into the system a strategy that belies any attempt to refute it. Every disagreement is dismissed with *ad hominem* of sorts, that the writer is hopelessly mired in bourgeois thinking. "Is it too much to demand that if he introduces subjective interpolations into his system they should be correct, well founded, and non-contradictory? And this reasonable demand Marx has continually contravened." This was Böhm-Bawerk's protest against the use of irrational assertions embedded in Marxist debate tactics.

Marxist theorist Rudolf Hilferding responded to Böhm-Bawerk in classic Marxist fashion. He dismissed the source, and with long-winded criticism tossed aside all of Marx's critics in the same way that Marx did. Concerning the great professor's detailed attempt to grapple with the details of Marx's theory, Hilferding writes:

> As spokesman for the bourgeoisie, it enters the lists only where the bourgeoisie has practical interests to defend. In the economico-political struggles of the day it faithfully reflects the conflict of interests of the dominant cliques, but it shuns the attempt to consider the totality of social relationships, for it rightly feels that any such consideration would be incompatible with its continued existence as *bourgeois* economics.[2]

As a member of the ruling class who is wedded to bourgeois ways of thinking, Böhm-Bawerk is just not capable of thinking the right away about these things. Because he thinks like a businessman, his mind is impervious to the truth—so there is no point in arguing with him. Instead, you should simply gain power, and then arrest him.

Closing Down the Debate

And so it goes today with so many political arguments. The rhetoric is on a much lower level, of course, but most political discussions on campus still follow this dismal script. Businessmen can't understand the logic of environmentalist thinking because they are out of touch with nature and its needs. Whites cannot comprehend the demands of black activists for affirmative action or reparations for slavery because the white experience and way of thinking blind them to the facts. And dissenters need not apply. When an eminent black economist (such as Thomas Sowell or Walter Williams) defends the free market, he is said to be "thinking like a white person." When a woman defends stay-home moms, or the rights of unborn children, she is dismissed by feminists as "not a real woman." This cheap tactic poisons the whole of modern politics. One may hardly even speak about the controversies of our time unless one belongs to the "victim group" being discussed. Even then, if a black person or a woman offers a dissenting point of view, he or she is dismissed as a patsy.

Arguing this way unravels the basis of all intellectual discourse. If we can't agree on the basic rules of evidence, all discussion is reduced to a series of demands followed by *ad hominem* attacks. We are reduced to the law of the intellectual jungle—a grim struggle for power among groups that cannot even really speak to each other. Is that compatible with a Christian view of society? Could any society, Christian or pagan, survive on such a basis?

Ludwig von Mises, the twentieth century's leading economist, himself understood that if we are to avoid this fate, there had to be some understanding and agreement on the rules we follow in honest argument. George Koether reports[3] that the first book Mises assigned his economics students was a logic textbook.[4] Things have only gotten worse since Mises taught; logic as a discipline is no longer part of high-school or even college study—which means that after sixteen years of formal schooling, hardly any students are taught even the basic rules of how to think. No wonder they are vulnerable to Marxist arguments.

The Reality Test: Marxism Flunks

Think of the Marxist regimes that have actually come to power over the decades: the old Soviet Union, Maoist China, Pol Pot's Cambodia, and today's North Korea. The consensus among scholars is that through political violence, starvation, and sickness these regimes killed at least 100 million people.[5] Marxism, everywhere it has been tried, has eliminated personal freedom, undermined the family, and rendered destitute everyone except a tiny Party elite. Orwell's novel *1984* was a truthful picture of the fruit of Marxist ideas.

We should not really be surprised at such a failure from a system which claims to explain all of human life in economic terms, but makes fundamental mistakes about how economics really works. Recall the examples cited above: Is a paper that someone spent twenty-four hours writing really worth eight times as much as a paper someone else wrote in three hours? For Marxists, it is. Now imagine running an entire economy on that basis—judging medical devices, for instance, by that standard. Is that the criterion you would use in choosing a doctor—that it took him twice as long to finish medical school?

Indeed, as the great economist and student of Catholic social teaching Wilhelm Röpke has said, "The purely economic basis of Marxism must be regarded today as merely an intellectual anachronism. Specifically, a suit is not eight times as valuable as a hat because it requires eight times as much labor as a hat to produce. It is because the *finished suit* will be eight times as valuable as the finished hat that society is willing to employ eight times as much labor for the suit as for the hat. It is upon this discovery that the remaining parts of Marxist theory (surplus value, capitalist disintegration) have foundered."[6]

So Marxism isn't practical. But is it still somehow moral? People used to say that communism was a "beautiful idea" that just wouldn't work in practice. Is that even true? Let's examine what Marxists say about the moral basis of economics. The Marxist theory of exploitation presumes that the gains of one group can only come *at the expense of another*. So if a law helps men, it must hurt women; if you sell something to someone, one of you is benefiting, and the other is being exploited. If you rent an apartment from a landlord, one of you is the aggressor, the other the victim. Is that really true? Would most of us be better off if we didn't trade things among ourselves, band together to work in common enterprises, invest in new businesses, or take jobs working for companies?

The economies that made Western prosperity possible were based on a mostly free market, and assumed that people make trades and contract employment because they *both expect to benefit*. Because we are all good at different things, the division of labor allows us to specialize in the jobs we are best at—instead of all trying to build our own houses, grow our own potatoes, and drill our own teeth. This free exchange and division of labor extends to all people regardless of sex, race, religion, or class. The pie is not fixed and divided but ever growing through human cooperation, the saving and investment of money, and the expansion of trade. While laws prevent fraud and theft, it is basically free cooperation and voluntary trade that produce what economist Frederic Bastiat called "economic harmonies."[7] We work together freely, and everyone benefits more than they would if the state controlled them and told each person what to do.

Thomas Jefferson's favorite economist, Count Destutt de Tracy, expressed this fact very clearly in his classic work *Treatise on Political Economy*:

> Society is purely and solely a continual series of exchanges. It is never anything else, in any epoch of its duration, from its commencement the most unformed, to its greatest perfection. And this is the greatest eulogy we can give to it, for exchange is an admirable transaction, in which the two contracting parties always both gain; consequently society is an uninterrupted succession of advantages, unceasingly renewed for all its members.[8]

When Things Really Do Get Ugly

Of course, we no longer live in Eden. Societies really do sometimes generate exploitative relationships. Apart from outright criminal behavior, this typically happens when some individuals manage to hijack the power of the government to skew the rules in their favor, or simply seize wealth from their neighbors. For instance, American slaves were not really property, but slave-owners used the power of the government to treat them that way. When a powerful company pressures the government into giving it a monopoly, or when one group gains legal privileges over another, we have a real example of exploitation. State-sponsored affirmative action is one excellent example. Laws that privilege one race, one religion, or one sex over another really do generate a group of victims, and teach people to think of themselves not as human beings with souls, but anonymous members of an angry group with grievances.

The use of government force amplifies and institutionalizes group conflicts. This is true as regards, for example, religion. Once the state begins to subsidize one form of religious expression, it convinces members of other religions that they are being ripped off, and the only means of defense is to organize and take back what is rightly theirs. This trajectory can become particularly explosive when it involves issues of race and sex, but conflict also appears in other areas, such as environmental and disability legislation. Invoking government power to gain an economic edge is the equivalent of pulling a gun in a bar fight. It raises the stakes, and makes everyone much more ruthless.

The very fact that so many of us look to the government to help us against our neighbors gives Marxism a false plausibility. It is not the case that ethnic groups are inherently in conflict. But it really can look that way, when instead of a free market in which all relationships in society are characterized by voluntary exchange and association, we hand forty or fifty percent of the national wealth over to the government to spend. Then instead of free and fair competition, it can seem like the best way to make a living is to organize into groups (often racially based) that can grab their "share" of the wealth. Politics divides people; markets bring them together.

For Fairness and Freedom

The Church has been very clear on the topic of Marxism and socialism more generally. In 1891, Pope Leo XIII wrote that "the main tenet of socialism, community of goods, must be utterly rejected, since it only injures those whom it would seem meant to benefit, is directly contrary to the natural rights of mankind, and would introduce confusion and disorder into the commonweal."[9] The pope was speaking here about the right to private property, which Marxism rejects. Denying this, he suggests, is the basis of violating natural rights and introducing social chaos. A century later, John Paul II pointed out that "class struggle in the Marxist sense and militarism have the same root, namely, atheism and contempt for the human person, which place the principle of force above that of reason and law."[10] This rejection of Marxism and socialist theory has implications for so-called "liberation theology," which baptizes a traditional Marxian view of economics with Christian moral theory. Many Catholics who speak up for "social justice," or who claim the mantle of Catholic social teaching, have in fact accepted the basic claims of Marxism—class struggle, the labor theory of value, and group consciousness. This leads them to completely misunderstand and misrepresent the proper concern which our popes have expressed for the needs of the poor, and to try replacing the Gospel's demand that we freely give to the needy with massive government programs that render Christian charity unnecessary.

Marxist morality has been condemned, authoritatively, by the Church. Marxist economics have been discredited by history. Every society that has followed Marx's prescriptions has sunk into a pit of envy, hatred, famine and tyranny. The real, Christian alternative to Marxism is the free society, which is rooted in what we might call cooperativism—that is, a society that protects the liberty of all people to form associations for their mutual betterment. Among those associations are families, churches, businesses, corporations, and civic associations. They all must be protected against the assaults of Marxists, who wrongly claim that these associations are secretly masking conflicts that only the state can resolve. That is the central message of Catholic social teaching, as reiterated by Pope Leo XIII (*Rerum Novarum*), Pope Pius XI (*Quadragesimo Anno*) and John Paul II (*Centisimus Annus*). It is also the ideal on which the American experiment was founded. The truths of faith, the conclusions of reason, and the evidence of history all agree in rejecting the envy-based ideology of Marxism. In whatever new guises it wears to tempt the unwary, we will know enough to reject it.

Jeffrey Tucker is editorial vice president of the Mises Institute, editor of www.mises.org, and author of thousands of essays and two books.

Recommended Reading

√ *The Economics of a Free Society,* by Wilhelm Röpke (Grove City, PA:
Libertarian Press, 1994).

√ *The Church and the Market: A Catholic Defense of the Free Economy,* by
Thomas E. Woods (Lanham, MD: Lexington Books, 2005).

√ *The Politically Incorrect Guide to Capitalism,* by Robert P. Murphy
(Washington, DC: Regnery Publishing, 2007).

√ *With God in Russia,* by Fr. Walter J. Ciszek and Daniel L. Flaherty (San
Francisco: Ignatius Press, 1997).

√ *Thank You for Arguing: What Aristotle, Lincoln and Homer Simpson
Can Teach Us About the Art of Persuasion,* by Jay Heinrichs (New York:
Three Rivers Press, 2007).

Notes

[1] Eugen von Böhm-Bawerk, *Karl Marx and the Close of His System*
(New York: Augustus Kelley, 1949).

[2] *Ibid.*

[3] *Austrian Economics Newsletter,* Volume 20, Number 3.

[4] Morris Cohen, *An Introduction to Logic and Scientific Method,* first
published in 1934.

[5] See Setephane Courtois et al., *The Black Book of Communism*
(Cambridge, MA: Harvard University Press, 1999).

[6] Wilhelm Roepke, *The Economics of a Free Society* (Chicago: Regnery,
1963), 18.

[7] Frederic Bastiat, *The Bastiat Collection: Volume 2* (Auburn, AL:
Mises Institute, 2007).

[8] Count Destutt de Tracy, *A Treatise on Political Economy* (Mises
Institute, 2009), 61.

[9] *Rerum Novarum,* no. 15.

[10] *Centesimus Annus,* no. 14.

Bonus Essay:

Commencement Heresy

"[Modernists] lay the axe not to the branches and shoots, but to the very root, that is, to the faith and its deepest fires…. [T]hey proceed to disseminate poison through the whole tree, so that there is no part of Catholic truth from which they hold their hand, none that they do not strive to corrupt."

– Pope St. Pius X

MODERNISM

John Zuhlsdorf

> Modernism is the theological tendency that alters
> or even rejects unchanging Catholic truths given
> to us by divine revelation, to adapt the Faith to the
> perceived needs and preferences of modern man.

Unlike other ideologies you encountered in this book, Modernism is pernicious precisely because it is elusive. To understand it we must start with a few distinctions. First, consider the term "modernism" as it is used in secular history and how it came to be the title for a heresy solemnly condemned by a pope. For the sake of convenience, I will refer to the broader cultural movement with a lower-case "m," and the heresy of Modernism with a capital "M."

From a secular point of view, modernism refers to a reaction to, and tendency away from, traditional forms of art, design, religious expression, political structures and anthropology, especially during the Industrial Revolution and into the twentieth century. Secular modernists pushed for a rupture with the past and with authority external to oneself. The result was experimentation, self-conscious shattering of conventions, the use of materials and artistic tools in unexpected ways, and divergence from traditional standards and authorities. In literature, think of names such as James Joyce and William Faulkner, in art Picasso and Mondrian.

This modernist movement had deeper historical roots. During the Renaissance, for example, there was a strain of humanism that promoted an overarching confidence in man's own powers apart from an external God, as well as an attitude of superiority over the ancients—whom humanists nevertheless studied and mined for models. This strain of humanism, together with new discoveries in the natural sciences, would fuel the subsequent movement that came to be called the Enlightenment. Everything could be sorted through man's own reasoning powers. The truth of things was to be sought not by authority or faith, but by the intellect and reason. In this view, man could, and should, free himself from the oppression of old, unenlightened governments, ways of life, and religions. Man should perfect himself and the world by his own efforts.

Results varied. For example, the American Revolution, rooted in the Enlightenment, founded an orderly republic. The French Revolution, on the other hand, drowned its ideals in blood.[1]

You Shall Be As Gods

A radical skepticism began to sweep away traditional certainties of the past. The French thinker René Descartes (+1650) had taught that we should abandon the authorities of the past, whose teachings contradict each other and leave us in confusion. We cannot trust what we experience with our senses, since the senses can deceive. We must find something we cannot doubt and make that a starting point. Ultimately, Descartes realized that what he didn't doubt was *the fact that he was thinking.* If he was thinking about his thinking, then he existed after all. In his 1637 *Discourse on Method,* he proposed the axiom, *"Je pense, donc je suis"* ("I think, therefore I am"), later refined into the oft-quoted *Cogito ergo sum.*

Descartes' mistake, and that of modernists after him, was to propose that one's subjective viewpoint become the measure of *all reality*, including divine revelation and morality. Everything is as it seems to *me*.

Inevitably, this approach to knowledge was applied to God. If our certainty about God's existence depends on our certainty about ourselves, then human reason becomes the final authority for what can be affirmed about God. At that point we lose sight of our creatureliness. We create a "god" in our own image and likeness. Descartes' erroneous solution isn't much different from the lie of the serpent, who told Adam and Eve: "You shall be as gods" (Genesis 3:5). This is what lies at the heart of modernism.

Among the results of small "m" modernism over the centuries were the undermining of the Church as a source of certainty and the exaltation of professors and "intellectuals." This seemed fitting, since secular modernism teaches that we must break with the past. Modernists hold that man should attain his goals entirely through this redefined reason. We make ourselves and the world better through our own efforts. We are the masters. We make all things new.

Modernism Rises in the Church

It was inevitable that the cultural currents dominating the secular world would influence the way Christians think about morality and theology. Slowly but surely, even within the Catholic Church, individual human reason was proposed as the ultimate criterion of truth, of good and evil. Truths of the Christian Faith became subject to the veto of reason. In the minds of some theologians, divine revelation had to be reshaped in accord with their own conclusions about human needs and progress. For these theologians, natural sciences and worldly philosophies became the starting point for theology. These men came to be called (and later to call themselves) "modernists."

Modernism in the Church is more of a mentality than a consistent body of doctrines. For the sake of critiquing it, however, the common tendencies of Modernism were systematized by the Church's teaching authority around that core error: the supremacy of secular reason.

The Church does not condemn human reason, reflection on the contents of divine revelation, man's technological advancement or even "modernity" per se. Rightly interpreted, all these are compatible with a life of Faith. But the Church does not, indeed cannot, accept human reason alone as the final authority over what we believe about God, divine revelation, or morality.

The Results of Modernism

In the face of rising Modernist ideas, both outside and inside the Church, Bl. Pope Pius IX, in *Syllabus of Errors* of 1846, condemned a list of Modernist propositions, especially the false notion that divine revelation itself ought to be subject to human reason or that its contents should change to accord with human progress.

In his 1907 encyclical letter *Pascendi dominici gregis*, Pope St. Pius X summed up Modernism as the "summary of all heresies." He names that "most disastrous doctrine of agnosticism" by which man is no longer governed by common sense, but is enslaved by his subjective sentiments, by his own experience. When an attempt is made to approach religion from this starting point, we end up by constantly revising even the most fundamental beliefs according to our culture and changing times. It would be as if the Faith were subject to an almost Darwinian evolutionism. At the end of this journey away from common sense and into the subjective we arrive at Relativism (see essay 2) and other errors that are toxic to Christian faith.

To see this religious approach put into practice, follow the history of the Anglican (Episcopal) church in the twentieth century. The Anglican communion largely embraced Modernist principles. That church followed the lead of popular sentiment in revising, one after another, its central tenets to suit modern man's "needs." In the 1930s, Anglicans legitimized the use of artificial contraception. In the 1970s, they approved ordination of women to their priesthood. In the 1980s, they endorsed the ordination of open and active homosexuals. That church seems now to be on the verge of celebrating same-sex "marriage."

The Magisterium of the Catholic Church once again rejected such a course when it condemned Modernism as a heresy, in particular in the aberrant propositions of two well-publicized theologians of the early 1900s, the French Fr. Alfred Loisy and the Irish Jesuit Fr. George Tyrrell, both of whom were excommunicated for refusing to accept correction from the superiors to whom they had publicly promised submission and obedience.

As a remedy to Modernism, Popes Leo XIII and St. Pius X advanced the study of scholastic philosophy as exemplified by St.

Thomas Aquinas. Popes also recommended the study of natural sciences, but in the light of revealed theology. All Catholic institutions were to be purged of anyone who openly espoused Modernism, and publications were to be carefully monitored. Every person entrusted with an ecclesiastical office was required to take the *Oath against Modernism*, which concluded solemnly, "This I promise, this I swear, so help me God."

The Thomistic revival urged by Pope Leo XIII proved for some decades successful, producing many neo-Thomist thinkers such as Etienne Gilson, Charles De Koninck, and the Dominican Fr. Reginald Marie Garrigou-Lagrange. But in the wake of the Second Vatican Council, and against the Church's explicit documents and law, the study of Thomistic philosophy gave way to secular philosophy in most Catholic universities and seminaries.

Modernism: The Sequel

The results of the Church's campaign against Modernism were mixed. On the one hand, Modernist influence was diminished in the short term. However, it went underground, only to emerge later, alive and well in many universities, theological faculties, chanceries, parishes, and, therefore, in the minds of many Catholics.

In the wake of the Second Vatican Council, intellectuals who secretly held to Modernist principles utilized the Council to disseminate their views. Theologians such as the pantheist Fr. Teilhard de Chardin and the anti-papal Fr. Hans Küng became popular among Catholics eager to be seen as trendy and up-to-date. In the name of Vatican II, though not in accord with the Council's actual teachings, Catholic education, pastoral life, and particularly liturgical worship were mutated by destructive changes which encouraged widespread disobedience, worldliness, and intellectual sloth.[2] Modernism resurged in a new and more virulent form.

If we were to try to sum up a single quality that marks the new face of Modernism, it would be *immanentism*. Immanence, from the Latin "to remain within," refers to a notion that divinity permeates the material universe, without transcending it. A radical immanentist would be not unlike a pantheist, holding that God is not personal but is rather a force found in everything. Putting it simplistically, think of "The Force" in *Star Wars,* or the "religion" of the Na'vi in *Avatar.*

Christians affirm that God is present to us. He is omnipresent. We also recognize that God entirely *transcends* the natural order. God is present because He chooses to be. By His presence God sustains the existence of the universe (not the other way around).

Many people today, even members of the Church, at least *formal* members, speak and act as if they believe in "The Force" instead of Almighty God who gave us the gift of the Church. Such a fuzzy notion of God, and self-confident feelings of being not so much "religious" as "spiritual," lulls people to allow their consciences to be formed on matters of serious moral importance (for example, premarital sex, fidelity, contraception, abortion, divorce and remarriage, cheating or theft, drug use, etc.), based on a personal sense of right and wrong often driven by the winds of popular trends or peer pressure. They barely consider the clear teachings of the Church, which speaks with the authority given her by Christ Himself. Such people usually won't deny the transcendence of God. They will even affirm it when it occurs to them or when pressed. Rather, they simply don't give much consideration to God as transcendent. They don't act as if He expects anything of us, or will judge us on our behavior. Nor do they pray as if they were addressing the eternal Creator and King of the universe.

This immanentism "lite" corrodes our view of who God is and who man is not. It chips away at our need for help from above. We spiral gently into neglect and indifference toward the supernatural order. We wrap ourselves up in our own little private worlds. We become less concerned with our guilt for sin, our absolute dependence on God for help through grace, our need for a Savior, and our approaching judgment. We neglect clarity in doctrine and submission to the Church's authority, given to her by Christ. The suggestion that something we might do could offend God and endanger our salvation becomes ever more remote. All this distorts our worship of God.

The Remedy
We cannot easily talk ourselves or others out of a Modernist mentality, so prevalent and comfortable. Most people won't

dedicate the time or have the inclination to work through arguments concerning the nature of God. We must instead learn to experience the presence of God as something alien and awesome. We must diligently seek encounters with the transcendent, with mystery.

The regular way to do this is through our reverent participation in authentic worship, in the Church's sacred liturgy.

Sadly, much of what passes as liturgy in the Catholic Church today is unworthy of the name, and directly contradicts the reforms called for by the Second Vatican Council. In many places, we find banal, narcissistic liturgies with little or no thought given to the God who is wholly other, mysterious, transcendent. Such worship is a thinly-veiled form of idolatry. Which strange gods are being worshiped? The lyrics of many of the songs used in church today give you a hint. The faithful are asked to sing about themselves, or to speak *as* God rather than *to* God. It sometimes seems that congregations have over the years slid into worshipping themselves. In his book *Looking at the Liturgy,* Aidan Nichols warns of the danger of "cultic immanentism"— that is, "the danger, namely, of a congregation's covert self-reference in a horizontal, humanistic world."[3]

A few years before his election as pope, Joseph Cardinal Ratzinger noted in his book *The Spirit of the Liturgy* that, as the Hebrews danced around their golden calf, they *knew* it was not God: they just wanted a less remote and less challenging deity. For modern man, who could be less challenging than oneself? Ratzinger wrote:

> Must we not admit that, at long last, under the incessant erosion of a modernist, immanentist mentality, especially in our worship, many people, regular church-goers among them, no longer even notice the calf, much less realize they made it in their own image?[4]

Fear not. A renewal of the Church's worship is underway. Pope Benedict XVI explicitly called for a new liturgical movement and it is gaining momentum. From a growing awareness of their deprivation, priests and long-suffering lay people have responded with enthusiasm. As Church leaders of previous generations retire or pass away, a new generation of bishops, priests, and lay leaders have started to guide

Catholic worship back into continuity with ancient traditions and obedience to Church documents. They are restoring our liturgical worship to a form that provokes a true encounter with the God who is mystery.

In his book *A New Song for The Lord*, Joseph Ratzinger observed that young people were reacting to the loss of mystery, rejecting the "banality and the childish rationalism of the pathetic homemade liturgies with their artificial theatrics."[5] Young people today don't want frauds. They want what Ratzinger calls the "true presence of redemption." This desire might lead more secularly inclined youth to the euphoria of rock concerts or drugs—anything which helps them rise above the banal. Ratzinger counters that "new places for faith emerge again where liturgy is lit up by mystery." In Ratzinger's view, mystery has "authority."

The most striking cure for the Modernist mentality in the world and in the Church is participation in liturgical worship that leads one past the instructional, the entertaining, the individualist or even the communal experience into *an encounter with Mystery*. The remedy for the self-centered, self-sufficient self-obsession of modern times is an experience akin to what William James[6] would call awe at transcendence, and Rudolph Otto[7] identifies as a religious sense of holy trembling that is nevertheless full of longing—which is the whole point of religion.

In vertical, God-centered worship, man has the opportunity to be stunned, shaken out of the ephemeral and the worldly, to pause in awe, in fear and longing at what he cannot understand and yet knows somehow to be true and necessary. While the older form of Holy Mass (i.e., the "Traditional Latin Mass") *explicitly* asks for surrender to the supernatural and strips us of our power to control, in more and more places—especially where the influence of Pope Benedict XVI's direction is being felt—the newer or Ordinary Form issued after the Second Vatican Council can also achieve this end if only it is celebrated with faithful reverence and obedience to the Church's rites as they actually are printed in the books.

Is this what your Sunday Mass offers you? If not, why not seek out something better? Find a more "traditional" parish, and attend its more solemn celebration of Mass, perhaps called a "sung" or "high" Mass. It may be that in your area there is a parish where you can participate in the traditional, Extraordinary Form of Holy Mass. You too can experience the liturgical worship which formed famous and unknown saints alike for centuries. This is your patrimony as a Catholic. This all belongs to you.

The difficult, demanding elements of worthy worship (kneeling, silence, obedience to formal ritual) create in the soul the tensions that are essential for an experience of mystery. This is our path out of the trap of Modernist self-absorption.

Worthy worship, properly oriented, puts you suddenly in the cave with Moses (see Exodus, chapter 33). Almost as a modern man might do, after learning God's Name, Moses demanded that He show Himself. So God told Moses to peer through a cleft in the rock to see just His *back* as He passed by: a glance of divine majesty ... but fleeting, indirect. In just such a way Christ's humanity both reveals and leaves hidden His Godhead.

Mystery must be our remedy, particularly in our prayer and the formal worship which must shape every aspect of our lives.

Rev. John Zuhlsdorf, a priest of the Suburbicarian Diocese of Velletri-Segni (Italy), is a convert from Lutheranism and was ordained in 1991 by John Paul II. His studies were in classical languages and Patristic Theology at the Augustinianum *in Rome. He is a regular columnist for the Catholic weekly* The Wanderer, *contributes to numerous publications, is an occasional TV commentator, and wrangles the popular blog* What Does The Prayer Really Say? *(www.wdtprs.com).*

Recommended Reading

√ *The Spirit of the Liturgy,* by Joseph Ratzinger (Pope Benedict XVI) (San Francisco: Ignatius Press, 2000).

√ *Newman Against the Liberals,* edited by Michael Davies (Devon, UK: Augustine Publishing Company, 1979).

√ *The Trojan Horse in the City of God,* by Dietrich von Hildebrand (Manchester, NH: Sophia Institute Press, 1999).

√ *The Popes against Modern Errors,* edited by Anthony J. Mioni (Charlotte, NC: St. Benedict's Press/TAN Books, 1999).

√ *Critics on Trial: An Introduction to the Catholic Modernist Crisis,* by Fr. Marvin O'Connell (Washington, D.C.: Catholic University of America Press, 1994).

Notes

[1]   See *French Genocide* by Reynald Secher (Notre Dame, IN: University of Notre Dame Press, 2003), which chronicles the savage persecution of the Catholic Church by the French revolutionaries, which claimed perhaps 300,000 lives.

[2]   Pope Benedict XVI, then Josef Cardinal Ratzinger, offered the best diagnosis of this phenomenon in the famous *Ratzinger Report* (San Francisco: Ignatius Press, 1985).

[3]   (San Francisco: Ignatius Press, 1996), 97.

[4]   (San Francisco: Ignatius Press, 2000), 23.

[5]   (New York: The Crossroad Publishing Company, 1996), 32.

[6]   *The Varieties of Religious Experience* (New York: Penguin Classics, 1982).

[7]   *The Idea of the Holy* (New York: Oxford University Press, 1958).

Will Your College Years Be a Waste of Time?

John Zmirak

L ife is short, but books are long. While the dull parts might seem to drag on endlessly, these four years you're spending in college will be over in a flash. Trust me. In a shockingly short time, you really will have to spend forty to seventy hours per week answering "urgent" emails, doing tedious research for lazy superiors, treading minefields of office politics, placating narcissists, and fetching older, fatter people coffee. Whatever your chosen field, it will be years before you get to the exciting parts. You can think of the intervening tediousness as apprenticeship, "paying your dues," or vocational hazing. But it won't be fun and it's going to last for years and years. While it's happening, you will find yourself so tired at day's end that you will rarely crack any of those unread Great Books you piled up in college and schlepped from one apartment to another. Instead, you will be proud of yourself for listening to National Public Radio or Fox News as you drift off into a nap. You know, just like your parents....

Never again will you have four consecutive years in which you are privileged, at other people's expense, to hang out in comfy lounges with coffee machines doing little but meditate on the meaning of life, the structure of history, the nature of man and how he can best live in community. This is your big chance to form your mind, shape it and test it in habits of clear and consistent thought. You really do have time now—as you probably never will again—to say something like: "People keep talking about how central Hegel is. I wonder what that's about. This book is four hundred pages ... okay, I'll give it a read."

So here's my message to students who want to make a difference in the world someday: Sign up for hard-core, serious courses and for the love of God do the reading. I wish I had. As a college professor now, I wouldn't be playing catch-up, racing through books I should have mastered when I was seventeen.

Choose your classes carefully. I edit a guide to hundreds of American schools called *Choosing the Right College*, so I can say this with some authority: Most college curricula are trash, including those at Ivy League universities. These school's bland "distributional requirements" assign equal value to courses like "Shakespeare's Tragedies" and "Godzilla in the Mist: Japanese Postwar Cinema." Unless you are attending one the Great Books schools, your college probably won't require you to master the fundamentals of Western civilization, where the Church took root and formed its doctrines. You will need to piece together such an education on your own.

Here's how to do it: Dig through your school's catalog to find a good course in each of eight fundamental areas—and, if possible, do all this before you pick a major. As my old friend and fellow writer Rod Dreher once told me: "I wanted to be a journalist, so I majored in journalism. Working in newspapers later on, I figured out that everything I ever really used in the profession I learned in my first semester. The other three years of journalism classes were a total waste of time—when I could have been learning something solid, to give me something to write about." Myself, I taught my liver way too much about the many varieties of gin. There might have been better ways to spend my time.

If you complete this do-it-yourself core curriculum, you will gain an edge in all your upper-level classes. You will be replicating, as best we can today, the education that informed America's founders. Most importantly, you'll deepen your understanding and appreciation for your Faith. So sign up for a course in each of the following:

1. Classical literature in translation. Homer, Cicero, Caesar—the fun stuff that ends up in footnotes to all subsequent literature through the centuries.

2. Ancient philosophy. Plato, Aristotle, all the way up through Boethius. Lay down the intellectual bedrock before you start on the sheetrock.

3. The Bible. Be careful about the professor here. You want your beliefs deepened and questioned, not put through a Vita Mix.

4. Christian thought before 1500. Here is your chance to read Augustine and Aquinas for credit.

5. Modern political theory. Where we went wrong, starting with Hobbes, up through Rousseau, Marx and Mill. Make sure you bring along the antidotes, in the form of Burke, Pope Pius IX, and Adam Smith.

6. Shakespeare. Avoid classes that mention "race," "class," or "gender." They will just ruin the Bard for you. And don't be afraid to rent DVDs in addition to reading—the plays were meant to be seen.

7. U.S. history before 1865. Our nation wasn't founded at Woodstock, no matter what they teach in high school.

8. Nineteenth-century European intellectual history. Most of the madness we are still suffering through today—and you have just read fourteen essays that scratch the surface—is a dumbed-down version of nineteenth-century errors. Read the addled geniuses who inspired contemporary maniacs, and learn how to spot false premises in seconds, instead of decades.

All this might sound ambitious, but it really isn't. It will fulfill most of your school's distributional requirements in a worthy way, and won't interfere with completing a major. As Mark Henrie writes in his short, fascinating *A Student's Guide to the Core Curriculum*, such a program is what most of the G.I.s returning from World War II had to master. The guys who wrote the classic TV series and Hollywood movies were educated in this style—hence all the references in Bugs

Bunny to Verdi and Wagner. That's why even the popular culture of previous decades stood at a much higher level than ... some of the textbooks you might be assigned in those pointless electives I am urging you to avoid. If you take the time to explore each of these intellectual areas, you are almost guaranteed to write smarter papers in your junior and senior seminars, do better applying to jobs or graduate school, and emerge as a sounder apologist for your Faith.

Seeking wisdom, you might wish to supplement the Great Books you will work through as part of your personal core curriculum with certain lesser known classics—for instance, the books you will find in the Recommended Reading section at the end of each essay here. You might find that some of those authors become your favorite writers, and form the basis for your research papers or your senior "capstone" project, if your school requires one. More importantly, these books—mostly by authors that modern academics long ago stopped reading—will set you free from the toxic intellectual trends that turn so many students into sheep.

Finally, on top of these classes and reading, it is critical to make friends who are open-minded and sympathetic. You needn't, and probably shouldn't, spend all your time with fellow believers. But most of us need at least some kind of support group with whom we can talk about doubts and difficulties. Beyond that, don't be afraid to mix it up intellectually with people whose ideas you find obnoxious. In my college years, the debating group where I spent most of my time—Yale's Party of the Right—was deeply divided between secular libertarians and orthodox Catholics. I learned a lot more countering, point by point, the tortuous arguments of programmatic atheists than I would have nodding cozily over cigars with the guys from the Latin Mass choir. I heartily recommend forming a reading group with folks who don't share all your premises, and honing your debating skills over lattes late into the night. You will be middle-aged, as I am, soon enough. You will have all your forties and fifties when you can catch up on your sleep.

About the Editor

John Zmirak graduated in 1986 from Yale University, where he studied religion and literature. He completed his MFA and Ph.D. in English at Louisiana State University, where he focused on Southern literature—especially the novels of Walker Percy. He is the author of five books so far, including *The Bad Catholic's Guide to the Seven Deadly Sins*, and the graphic novel *The Grand Inquisitor*. He is editor of CollegeGuide.org and the biannual print guide *Choosing the Right College*. He writes regularly for InsideCatholic.com and other periodicals, and is currently writer-in-residence and assistant professor of literature at Thomas More College in Merrimack, N.H. He is the proud father of two beagles, Susie and Franz Josef.